ALSO BY MAYA SHANBHAG LANG

*The Sixteenth of June*

# What We Carry

# What We Carry

A MEMOIR

## Maya Shanbhag Lang

THE DIAL PRESS

New York

Published in the United States by The Dial Press, an imprint of Random House, a division of Penguin Random House LLC, New York.

THE DIAL PRESS is a registered trademark and the colophon is a trademark of Penguin Random House LLC.

Library of Congress Cataloging-in-Publication Data
Names: Lang, Maya, author.
Title: What we carry: a memoir / by Maya Shanbhag Lang.
Description: First edition. | New York: The Dial Press, [2020]
Identifiers: LCCN 2019018845 | ISBN 9780525512394 (hardback) |
ISBN 9780525512400 (ebook)
Subjects: LCSH: Lang, Maya. | Lang, Maya—Family. | Women authors, American—Biography. | East Indian American women—Biography. | Mothers and daughters—United States—Biography.
Classification: LCC PS3612.A55425 Z46 2020 | DDC 813/.6 [B]—dc23
LC record available at https://lccn.loc.gov/2019018845

Printed in the United States of America on acid-free paper

randomhousebooks.com

2 4 6 8 9 7 5 3 1

First Edition

Book design by Debbie Glasserman

For my mother. Both versions.

And for my daughter, who lights the way.

*Illusion is the first of all pleasures.*

—VOLTAIRE

*We tell stories in order to live.*

—JOAN DIDION

*You your best thing, Sethe. You are.*

—TONI MORRISON

# Prologue

"*Mayudi,* I want to tell you a story," my mother told me.

My daughter was nine days old. Overwhelmed by the new demands of motherhood, I had turned to my mom for support. I wanted her to listen in her sympathetic way, to take up my feelings, to murmur in agreement as she did. Always, after talking to my mom, I felt better.

"Once," she began, "there was a woman in a river. She held a child in her arms, her son—"

"Wait," I interrupted, puzzled, "is this an Indian story? A myth?" I wondered if my mom was about to launch into a Hindu legend involving Lakshmi or some other goddess struggling in the Ganges.

"Just listen," my mom admonished. She cleared her throat.

"Once," she began again, "there was a woman in a river. She held a child in her arms. Her son. She needed to cross the river, but it was much deeper than expected. As the water reached her chest, she panicked.

"She saw that she had a choice. She could save herself or she could save her child. They would not both make it. What does she do?"

Listening, I felt restless. I didn't know what this riddle had to do with me or why my mom was telling it. Besides, I knew the answer without having to give it much thought. The woman would sacrifice herself for her child. It was how all stories of motherhood went, particularly Indian myths. I said so to my mother, expecting her to agree. But she surprised me.

"We do not know the outcome," she told me. "We do not know what the woman in the river chooses. Until we are in the river, up to our shoulders—until we are in that position ourselves, we cannot know the answer. We tell ourselves we will sacrifice ourselves for our children, but the will to live is very strong."

Her words astonished me. A woman choosing herself! The mere possibility felt audacious.

"We must not judge," my mom continued. "That is the real lesson of the story. Whatever a woman decides, it is not easy."

This wasn't how my mother usually spoke. She had sacrificed everything for her children, a fact she liked to allude to as often as possible. Hearing her acknowledge maternal selfishness was jarring. Strangely, though, it comforted me.

Practical by nature, a scientist by trade, my mom usually simplified matters, boiling them down to their essence. Forthright, blunt, she was the person who had all the answers, who did not suffer from self-doubt, yet here she was, acknowledging nuance and the possibility that life might be more complicated than easy answers permit.

I wasn't sure what to make of this new side of her. While part of me welcomed it, I was an exhausted new mother. I wanted her to cut to the chase: to tell me how to manage motherhood, to describe what she had done. I wanted her to be who she had always been. When I most craved clarity, she had given me an enigma.

I didn't understand that she was trying to give me the answers I sought. She just didn't know how. Her attempt was circuitous and clumsy. Instead of being blunt, she was being coy.

In the years to come, I would often think of the woman in the river, up to her chest in rising waters, paralyzed by fear and indecision. Eventually, as I learned the truth about my mother's choices, I would see my family's story captured in the tale. I had been right to be restless when my mom first told me that story. I had known on some level that she was being evasive. What I hadn't realized was that, through fiction, she was trying to come clean.

The story was her way of owning up to what she had long hidden—to help me see what had always been before my eyes.

I

# 1

&#10047;

I am six months pregnant, living in a city that feels utterly alien to me, talking on the phone, as I so often do, with my mother. Talking to her makes me feel less isolated, more assured, though on this particular day our conversation takes a strange turn.

"I am thinking of taking an easier job," she says, "now that I am old."

"Mom," I scoff, "you're not old."

"Soon I will be sixty-five."

"That's two years away!"

"I must face reality. I can no longer be who I was."

I go quiet, unsure if I am supposed to argue with her or not.

My mom has a history of abrupt decisions. Ten years earlier, when I was in college, she divorced my dad after nearly thirty years of marriage, a shock to our Indian family. She quit her job and moved from Long Island to the unknown suburbs of New Jersey. These decisions weren't bad ones—I'd wanted her to divorce my dad for some time—but they were startling for the way she did them, all at once. "Why New Jersey?" I asked from my dorm room. It was all I could think to say. "It will be good for work," she replied. She was right. She landed a dream position running clinical trials for pharmaceutical companies and was happier than I had ever seen her.

However perplexing, her decisions have always worked out.

Who am I to doubt her? When I was a girl, there was once a car accident on our street, a motorcyclist flung onto a neighbor's lawn. My mom rushed outside and took control of the scene. This is how I picture her, a doctor radiating authority, even in a nightgown. She is the most capable person I know. I may not always understand her, but I have complete faith in her.

A week after that phone call, she gives notice. Her boss is stunned. He offers to reduce her hours, eliminate travel, hire assistants, all to no avail. She has already applied for a position at a state hospital. "A state hospital!" her boss cries. "You'll be bored to tears!"

My mom sounds pleased when she shares his reaction with me. She is up against a wall no one else can see, which is more or less her ideal state.

"What if you don't get the job at the hospital?" I ask nervously.

"I will get it."

"Is this what you want?"

"It is not what I want. It is what I *need*."

Such are my mother's pronouncements.

"But why?" I press. "You're giving up your dream job."

"This way I will have a pension. If I am ever in a nursing home, those places are so expensive, you would not believe."

Off she goes citing statistics. I picture her absorbing the numbers through her reading glasses. She is farsighted: eyes like a hawk for distance, but unable to see anything up close. This applies not only to reading.

An immigrant, she came to this country for her children. Throughout my childhood, she fixated on the costs of sending me and my brother to college. If my outgrown jeans showed ankle, she told me to wear longer socks. "Everyone at school thinks I'm poor," I mumbled. "Let them think that," she snapped.

"Their parents will have credit card debt to go with their nice jeans."

In the distance, she sees her goals. She funnels herself toward them. She scowls if anyone suggests alternatives. Help and convenience are to be batted away.

A few days later, she gets the job at the state hospital, just as predicted. This is the thing about my mom: She may be cryptic, but she is always right.

"I don't know if I should congratulate you," I confess.

"This is for the best."

"Maybe you'll be able to visit me more, with a less demanding job."

She chuckles. "That would be nice. What matters is my pension. I do not want to burden my children!"

So it goes between us. Everything she does is for my benefit. This is what a mother's love looks like to me. It looks like suffering.

I accept it. I am about to become a mom three thousand miles away from her, in a gray, drizzly city that feels wholly unfamiliar. Soon, I will be the one putting my needs last. It helps to believe that somewhere in the world, I still come first.

# 2

Before moving to Seattle, my husband, Noah, and I lived in Manhattan. We had grown tired of the city—exorbitant rents, minuscule apartments—and were at a crossroads in our careers.

I was about to complete my PhD in comparative literature. I was no scholar, but I was happy enough pretending to be one. I got to read books all day. It felt like a grand luxury.

I wasn't sure, however, what to do with my degree. I didn't want to apply for tenure-track positions. I'd wanted a PhD for the same reason I'd ever done anything: to be impressive. At twenty-eight, I had a series of stints behind me. I'd been pre-med, then a management consultant, then an academic. I had leapt from one role to the next. None fit.

Noah, four years older than me and from Southern California, was working as a lawyer at a big firm, a glamorous-sounding job he loathed. He hated watching partners yell at secretaries, the lack of women and minorities in positions of power, and the fact that many of the companies he defended (tobacco and chemical conglomerates) deserved, in his mind, to be sued. Noah's conscience was one of the reasons I fell for him. He grew up poor. He didn't want his future kids to go without health insurance the way he had. His pragmatism and conscience butt heads in his work.

The funny thing is that because Noah grew up poor and Jew-

ish, we understood each other perfectly, though I had been neither of those things. He understood why I felt guilty buying a
nice pair of jeans. I understood why he felt excluded at Christmas. We had both been shaped by guilt and frugality and a
complicated shame. We were the kids who had shown up to
school with our textbooks wrapped in brown paper bags. We
knew what it was like to be on the outside, looking in.

We also learned what it was like to be on the inside, looking
out. We had escaped our pasts. Noah's family never expected
him to put himself through law school or move to New York
City. My Indian parents never imagined that it was acceptable
to read books all day. We had proved them wrong. We had made
it. Yet no matter how impressive our jobs (a lawyer at a big firm)
or achievements (a PhD at twenty-eight), we felt like misfits. We
didn't really belong.

When Noah was offered a job as in-house counsel at Nin-
tendo while I defended my dissertation, the timing seemed perfect. Here was a chance for him to join a feel-good company, for
us to leave Manhattan, and, best of all, for me to duck the question of what to do with my life. We were moving across the
country! It was like being handed an alibi.

We packed our small apartment into our car and headed
west. Our dog, Lola, a black Lab mix, sniffed curiously at the
fresh air from the back seat. We had just put an offer on a house,
something we had no experience doing. We were filled with
conjecture about what it would be like to be homeowners. Any
concerns came from Noah. I was in charge of the giddiness.
"Relax!" I told him. "We're going to love it."

Were we? He raised some good points. We didn't know Seattle well. I had pushed us into buying a house because I wanted
something to show for myself. When friends said, "You bought
a house *already*?" I felt a little better.

I didn't have a job. I didn't have a plan. Beneath my enthusiasm, I was filled with doubt. Never before had I uprooted like this. It was the sort of all-in move my mom would make. I thought about how her gambles always worked out. I wanted to believe that if I sounded confident the way she did, if I laughed off concerns, I would land on my feet just like her.

# 3

⚜

On a sunny day, Seattle is a glittering emerald: endless ever-greens, panoramic views of the water, ridged mountains cleaving the sky. Noah and I gape at the sheer beauty. A trip to the drugstore can turn cinematic, snowcapped mountains shining in the distance.

It is a city of books and coffee and dogs. Recycling is embarked upon with gusto. Citywide composting means that food scraps get turned into fertilizer. Whole parks exist for Lola's pleasure. Styrofoam is outlawed, as are plastic bags. Washington becomes one of the first states to legally approve gay marriage. All of this makes us proud.

The culture of the Pacific Northwest is a sharp contrast to that of New York. The ethos is one of outdoorsy eccentricity: socks with sandals, canvas tote bags, recumbent bikes. Tech executives worth millions look vaguely homeless or like they've just completed an outdoor race.

I meet a former dot-commer who now tends goats. A neighbor, a thin wisp of a man, leads workshops on movement. "Movement?" I ask, confused. "Movement!" he affirms. At a party, I talk to a woman who left her job at Microsoft to sell crystals. She wears a kaftan and speaks effusively, each gesture of her arms sending forth wafts of patchouli.

I want to love this progressive city, but I find myself feeling out of sorts. While I appreciate Seattle's lack of pretense, it isn't a terribly diverse place. I'm pretty sure I singlehandedly double the number of minorities in our neighborhood. The East Coast may have its flaws, but I miss it, a tug of the heart I recognize as homesickness.

To keep busy, I start working for an animal rescue group. I justify it to myself as a stepping-stone to a new career in non-profits. I prepare a whole spiel to defend it, but in this new city, no one asks to hear it.

When I find out I'm pregnant, Noah and I are ecstatic. I am also relieved. Here is temporary shelter from the grand question. I won't have to reinvent myself. The baby can be a way of buying myself more time.

# 4

My mom and I talk often, sometimes daily. Part of me keeps waiting for her to question my choices and say, "I didn't send you to a fancy college to be a dog lady!" or, "Is this really how you want to use your PhD?" She never does. She isn't that person.

She is my first phone call, the one who makes any piece of news real, any achievement official, any blow less painful. The mere act of greeting each other can cause us both to laugh. "Hi, Mom!" I sing the words. My joy at getting her on the line is palpable, like an addict getting hold of a drug.

Having spent most of her career as a psychiatrist, she has an exquisite way of listening. She asks about each part of my day, no detail too small. If I tell her I need to go grocery shopping, she wants to know the name of the market, how far it is, if I like it there, so that I am left with the pleasant sense that she is with me.

When I give her the spiel about the nonprofit, she says, "That makes sense," her voice full of approval. When I tell her about the goat man and the patchouli lady, she laughs appreciatively. When I share my doubts about Seattle, she listens thoughtfully.

"Hi, Mom!" The two syllables open a magic door, sympathy and understanding on the other side. I love when she picks up. I don't bother hiding it. When she picks up, I am home.

She reacts to me the same way. If it's been a few days since we last spoke, she bursts out, *"Mayudi, Shanudi, Ranudi!"* It is a nonsense rhyme in Marathi—little Maya, my sweetheart, my queen—the three words lining up like cherries on a slot machine.

My mom and I laugh gaily, basking in our shared affection. She knows what she means to me. I know that she knows. It pleases us both—mom and daughter, in need of nothing and no one else.

# 5

<br>

When I was four, my mom took me to the dentist. We had just moved to Long Island from Queens. The dentist was white and handsome, a novelty to me. Accustomed to Indian faces and to speaking Marathi, I felt shy in his presence.

As he examined my teeth with gloved hands, he tried to engage my mom in conversation. "Are you folks from India?" he asked. "You speak Hindi?" He pronounced *Hindi* the American way, which I had never heard before, causing me to giggle. He frowned and reached up to adjust the light.

"New gloves!" my mom barked.

"Excuse me?"

"You have broken sterile technique by touching the light. You must change your gloves."

He blinked, then smiled. "Listen, miss, I've been in practice for many years—"

"Did you disinfect that light after your last patient? This is a young child. You must change your gloves. And I am not 'miss,' I am a doctor."

Reddening, he slowly removed the gloves and reached for new ones.

Not ten minutes later, she corrected him once more: "New gloves!"

Something transpired that day. I left the dentist's office with my head held high.

Six months later, when we returned for my checkup, the dentist looked cowed. "Dr. Shanbhag," he said, "I—I disinfected the light."

My mother did not change for others; she caused others to change for her. In her fierceness, I felt her love. She was my advocate. She did not care what people thought of her. She cared about what mattered: me.

After my parents divorced, my mom put a hundred thousand miles on her car in a few short years. I'm pretty sure most of those miles came from visiting me and my brother.

She hopped in her car at the drop of a hat. If I so much as coughed on the phone, there she would be at my doorstep, her car stuffed full with various items: a pot of lentil soup, Swiffer Dusters, a twelve-pack of paper towels I couldn't fit in my tiny closet, a wide-spectrum antibiotic (just in case), a two-pound container of cookies, boxes of Claritin. She was like a traveling representative from Costco.

Once, while I was in grad school, I complained to her about my aching lower back. I wasn't sure how I was going to finish my final papers when sitting aggravated the pain. "You should get a comfortable chair!" she scolded. I laughed. I had neither the time nor the budget to go furniture shopping. Besides, my brother in Boston had promised me his old recliner, one that tilted at just the right angle to make typing on my laptop a joy. After finals were behind me, I figured I'd find a way to get the chair.

The very next afternoon, I heard a knock at my door. Opening it, I was stunned to see the recliner—and, behind it, my exhausted mom. She had driven to Boston, picked up the chair, and come straight to me in New York.

"Mom, all that driving in one day—that's crazy!"

She shrugged. "You needed the chair. What else am I going to do on a Sunday?"

"But that thing's heavy! I don't understand how you carried it."

She smiled. "I am your mother. That is how."

For the next two weeks, as I crammed to finish my term papers, that recliner was my oasis, the only place I could sit without being in agony. Each time I settled into it with relief, I imagined my mother lugging the chair to my door, insisting that it was nothing. She was not sentimental or effusive, had never read to me as a child or baked me cookies, but she would travel great distances for me and carry astonishing weights. When I most needed her, she was there.

Noah and I had been out for a walk on a glorious June day when we came back to our apartment, pressed Play on our home answering machine, and heard the news of my friend Jared's death.

I froze.

My friend from college, Jared had been battling cancer. I had spoken with him just the previous week, assuring him he would beat the disease, sharing a recipe for a healthful soup. How foolish I felt as that voicemail played.

In that moment, time stopped. The walls of the apartment closed in around me. "Honey—" Noah began, but I shook my head violently and turned away from him. Without a word, I ran into the bedroom.

There was only one person I wanted then.

"Oh!" my mom cried out when I shared the awful news. Her voice was anguished. "Oh no! This cannot be. He was so young!"

As she gave voice to each sentiment ("He was so brilliant and kind! Oh, life is not fair. How could this happen to someone so good?"), my tears fell. Each statement she voiced peeled back a layer of my own emotions: the injustice of Jared's death, my incomprehension that he could be gone.

It was a release to have her say what I could not. This was why I loved my mom, why I craved her audience, why only she would do. In life's most difficult moments, there was no wall between us. She would never say, "I'm so sorry for your loss," would never put herself on the other side of hardship. She came over to my side. She ached for me, felt for me. She received life's blows on my behalf.

"Do you need me to come to you?" she asked. "I can get in my car right now—"

"No, Mom, it's okay."

"I want you to call me," she said sternly. "You must not hesitate! Even if it is the middle of the night, even if you are calling for no reason. Do you understand? Do not worry about bothering me, *Mayudi*."

I smiled a little, tasted salt.

Only then, after I had spoken with her, did I feel ready to face Noah and the world beyond, a world in which my friend no longer lived, a world that could be unjust and cruel, where life continued, though it should have stopped in my friend's honor. Only after talking with my mom could I begin to process what had happened. Her listening ear made life register. Because of her, I felt less alone.

# 6

When I was a kid, my mom often discussed her patients with me. Maybe she did so because they were on her mind, or maybe she knew how much I liked hearing the stories. I couldn't believe people's problems: the inability to leave the house without touching the sidewalk seven times, the voice of God in a lightbulb. It was like being let in on a secret: Grown-ups struggled.

Her patients came to her after their medications failed. They came to her after being told they were imagining the side effects. They came to her when they were at their wits' end.

She came home furious about their mistreatment. Hastily scribbled scripts, unnecessarily high dosages, the mountain of problems resulting from a simple misdiagnosis: These enraged her. She had little patience for other psychiatrists who didn't understand the newest medications. She had tremendous sympathy for her patients' plights. She sided with them, always.

This pleased me. I liked thinking of her as a champion of the underdog because it meant there was hope for me as the underdog of the family. Home life revolved around my brother and my dad. Eight years older than me, my brother had important tests to study for. I was to be quiet and stay out of his way. My father asserted himself as the patriarch. My mom earned more money than him and was the true head of household, but this was never to be acknowledged. She cooked his meals and ironed his shirts and washed his socks, a swirl of black in the basement sink. She and I listened politely whenever he rehearsed presentations for his job as an engineer. He never asked about my mom's job. She spoke of it only to me.

My dad had a temper. I became his main target after my brother left for college when I was ten. "Worthless girl," he would mutter.

He told me that men are smarter than women. "That is why most inventions come from men," he would say. When I'd point out that women haven't been given as many opportunities, he'd retort, "What is the reason for that? Because they aren't as *smart.*"

Against this backdrop, my mom's stories provided a glimpse of an alternate universe where people weren't worthless; they were simply misunderstood. My dad would never sympathize with the need to touch the sidewalk seven times, any more than he understood why I read novels ("garbage," he called them). To him, I was useless. To her, no one was a lost cause.

She and I took refuge in science. We discussed bipolar disorder and schizophrenia, neurotransmitters and the postsynaptic gap. I learned that pharmaceutical companies often put $x$ and $z$ in product names (Xanax, Paxil, Zoloft, Prozac) because it makes them more memorable. I learned that my sixth-grade math teacher, who wept during quizzes, probably had undiagnosed depression. I learned that people's insides were more complicated than their outsides revealed.

Being out with her at the mall or supermarket was like being with a celebrity. People came running up to us. "Dr. Shanbhag!" they cried. "You don't understand," they would say, turning to me. "Your mother saved my life. Your mother is *amazing.*" Their eyes were emphatic. "Do you get it?" they seemed to say. "Do you see how wonderful she is?"

While patients thanked her profusely, my mom chuckled. "It's just the medication," she would remark after the person walked away.

Yet always, always, there was a story: the guitar player who turned manic when placed on the wrong antidepressant; the severely dyslexic teenager misdiagnosed as schizophrenic; the single father of two committed to a psychiatric ward against his will despite not posing a threat to himself or his children. To give them the right diagnosis, she had to listen. I knew she was being modest when she suggested otherwise. I knew from my own experience that she listened with exquisite care.

# 7

A couple of months before my due date, she calls me. "I can come for one week when the baby is born. After that, I am not so sure."

"What do you mean, Mom?"

"My new job has strict policies. I will not have vacation days for some time, maybe a year."

"A *year*? But . . . I thought the point of this job was to make your life easier."

"The point is for me to earn a pension," she corrects.

Money. It is her constant preoccupation. When I was a girl, she often worked late at night, picking up extra shifts at hospitals like a waitress looking for tips.

Being the offspring of Indian working professionals offers a strange conundrum. She was a doctor, my dad an engineer, yet a casual observer would be forgiven for thinking us penniless. We certainly lived that way.

We didn't have cable TV. We didn't own books. When kids at school alluded to sitcoms or video games, I had no idea what they were talking about. I eyed their clothes with envy. I sensed a world of pleasure just beyond reach, one where families ate at restaurants and sought entertainment and went on vacation. We did none of those things. Our only trips were to India, which were trips of obligation, not pleasure. We visited relatives and dispensed goods from a Samsonite suitcase that had been stuffed full for this purpose.

On the nightly news, I saw that India was part of the third world, a place of poverty. I didn't know how to reconcile this with my experience. Our life in America was one of austerity. In India, we lived like royalty. I had fond memories of my maternal grandparents' home in Bombay, the elevator a filigreed bird-cage, the marble tile elaborate and cool to the touch. Servants prepared lavish meals. My grandparents gave me gold jewelry. Our upper-caste status meant that we were treated with defer-ence. This embarrassed me, but my mom was accustomed to it. In India, she transformed into someone relaxed and carefree. It was like seeing a princess returned to her castle.

On Long Island, that ease vanished. Lines creased my moth-er's forehead. Worry hung over the house. When teachers asked me to describe India, I gathered they didn't want to hear my actual stories. "Were there lepers?" one asked in a whisper. I shared this with my mother, who laughed darkly. "People in this country don't really see us," she said.

I didn't understand what she meant. I didn't recognize that my parents were foreigners who felt out of their element in the anonymous white suburb where we lived. I took the problem to be my mom's most frequent topic of conversation: money.

On Mondays, she worked until ten o'clock at night. I would listen for her car from my bedroom and then race downstairs to open the garage. The clicker was broken. I figured we didn't have the funds to fix it. It was the only way to explain why, at the age of eight, I was relied upon to scramble down the stairs and let her in, no matter that the car that pulled into the garage was a luxury sedan.

Such choices made perfect sense in my parents' universe. They reasoned that expensive cars were more reliable. Why else would they cost more? They didn't know how to go about getting a garage opener fixed. They regarded the Yellow Pages with a mix of apprehension and dread: an American invention filled with opportunities to be ripped off and cheated. Unsocial people, they didn't talk to the neighbors. The outside world was perilous.

The legacy of this is that I have a sometimes-uneasy relationship with money and an always-uneasy relationship asking for help. "Were you raised during the Depression or something?" a roommate once asked, staring as I scraped a jar clean. "Why didn't you come to me?" my dissertation advisor asked, exasperated, when he found out I'd been trying to teach myself ancient Greek for my research. "I could have set you up with a tutor!" Thrift and self-reliance had been drilled into me.

In Seattle, after becoming pregnant, I decide I will be a stay-at-home mom. "I thought you were going for a career in non-profits," Noah says, surprised. I explain that if I work, we will lose money. Nannies and daycare cost a fortune. Noah has hefty student loans from college and law school. I can tell he finds my answer odd. My worry about money is sometimes too much, even for him.

To my mother, the decision makes perfect sense. I savor her approval. This is my first taste of motherhood. I like how self-sacrifice feels, clean and pure. My task as a mother will be to curtail convenience and desire. "It is not what I want," I nearly say to Noah. "It is what I *need*."

# 8

As motherhood looms, I begin to experience a walk-the-plank dread. Excited as I am to meet the baby, I have certain other feelings I've been keeping to myself. I'm frightened, but as a mom I'm not supposed to feel that way. I'm supposed to intuitively know how to handle an infant. I feel isolated, but I'm not supposed to feel that way, either. I'm supposed to radiate contentment. I don't know how I internalized these messages. I only know that when people elbow Noah and say, "How are you? Nervous? Scared?" I want them to do it to me.

I think back to when my nieces were born, how my mom and I visited my brother and his wife every other weekend. "New parents need support!" my mom would bellow, pushing her way through their front door. Whether or not our presence was desired with such frequency, there we were, cooking, folding laundry, babysitting, delighted by our new roles as grandma and aunt.

I don't have any family in Seattle. Any local friends are new. On weekends, I cook meals and freeze individual portions. I stock the pantry. I'm preparing for motherhood the way one braces for a storm.

What troubles me is that I don't know what to picture. I knew how to excel at school and work because my mom's stories of medical school and residency had given me a template. When I ask her about motherhood, however, she grows terse.

"How did you handle the sleep deprivation?" I ask.

"You and your brother slept through the night."

"Even when we were newborns?"

"I was lucky."

"With labor . . . did you get an epidural?"

"No, it did not hurt."

Even to my gullible ears, these answers sound suspicious.

Determined to bond with my unborn daughter, I decide to write her letters. I buy a notebook and a nice pen. I think ahead to when she is eleven or twelve. I want her to have evidence of how loved she is.

The letters I write feel purposeful but strange. I am writing across time from my current self to her future self. By the time she reads the letters, I will have already formed in her mind as a mom. I wonder if I'm actually doing her a disservice, if instead of feeling loved and reassured, she'll see right through me. "Who the heck were you?" she'll say. "This doesn't sound like you at all."

I realize that the letters aren't really for her. They're for me. Writing has always been my coping mechanism. I'm trying to forge my way into this next chapter of my life.

There is the current me (unformed) and then there is the future me (the mom). I don't yet know who that person is. I know who I want her to be: nurturing, loving, adept, someone who bakes pies and gives the best hugs, who reads stories and sings songs. This person feels utterly fictitious.

I can't see into the future the way my mom did. Her trajectory was a straight line. She became a doctor at the age of twenty-three. She chose psychiatry because it offered family-friendly flexibility. She had planned for me before I was even born.

I don't know how to become someone whose choices add up coherently. This is what terrifies me. My daughter needs someone who has answers. I have nothing but questions.

# 9

On a brilliant, sunny day in February, a day when the clouds seem to part just for the occasion, I give birth to my daughter, a moment so overwhelming in its dazzling intensity that I feel certain of the presence of some divine force that has led to this, the beautiful, perfect baby in my arms.

Gazing at her, I laugh with joy and relief. Noah and I wipe tears from each other's faces. "You were amazing," he says. "That was *amazing*."

We decide to name her Zoe, which I know from my study of ancient Greek means "life," not in its somatic form (*bios*), but in its glorious and teeming fullness. What better name could there be for my daughter?

Though I'm ecstatic, some part of me is also uneasy because of the events preceding Zoe's arrival. At the hospital, a resident told me I was zero centimeters dilated when I was six centimeters along, meaning I wasn't admitted when I should have been. The nurse who inserted my catheter forgot to empty it. She and another nurse had a good laugh about this while I threw up.

It wasn't just the hospital experience that weighed on me. While I labored, Noah kept worrying over his parking spot. "Do you want to check on the car?" I finally asked. Relieved, he hurried off. He hadn't exactly been by my side the way I'd envisioned.

I tell myself that the mistaken resident and the bad nurse

were flukes, that Noah had simply been anxious. Everything will be fine. It has to be. As adrenaline gives way to exhaustion, I ask a nurse if Zoe can spend a few hours in the hospital nursery. "Oh no, we encourage co-sleeping here," the nurse answers. "Oh," I say, faltering, "but I—I haven't slept at all. I think I need, you know, to rest." The nurse frowns. "Your labor was easy. No complications. You'll learn to nap when the baby naps." I look to Noah, who shrugs.

The next day, no one checks on me. Tests and pokes and prods abound for Zoe. I'm told to make an appointment with my doctor in six to eight weeks.

Once, years ago, I went to the ER for stitches, a minor injury over which they made a big fuss: care instructions, a mandatory follow-up. Now, there are no care instructions, even though, this time, I have stitches in a far more sensitive place.

When I get home, lugging the car seat through the door, the house is dark. I unearth my portions from the freezer to make dinner while Noah goes to get Lola from the boarding kennel. As I watch the soup rotate in the microwave, I call my mom. "What do you mean, you're home?" she demands. "You gave birth yesterday! Are you in bed? What is that beeping? You must rest!"

Hearing her reaction, I realize that this is what I wanted: an advocate. I picture my mom yelling at the nurses and the resident, the way she once did with my childhood dentist. She never cared if she was being rude. She cared about getting me the right care.

My first week as a mom is a struggle. My milk is slow to come in. Zoe won't take a bottle. Her weight drops by more than 10 percent—a red flag. One terrifying day, she doesn't produce enough wet diapers or respond to stimuli and, dehydrated, requires medical attention. Never before have I felt like a failure. I can't meet her basic needs.

"Am I doing a bad job?" I ask my mom over the phone. "Because it feels like I am."

"No! Why would you think such a thing? American doctors are a joke. Making you count diapers! You just need to hang in there. I will be there soon."

She and my brother are scheduled to visit together the following week. I'm elated at the prospect of seeing them. Zoe doesn't yet do anything, but the thought of my mom and brother meeting her means the world. It is a powerful realization and a disheartening one. I want my family most now that they're three thousand miles away.

# 10

My brother and I weren't close growing up, but our once-insurmountable age difference now proves insignificant. While he can only stay for the weekend, the help he provides is considerable. He zips off to the store to replenish the fridge, assembles the baby swing I haven't had a chance to unpack, and brings me glass after glass of water, somehow divining I am thirsty. "How'd you know?" I ask, gulping it down. He shrugs. "It makes sense, I guess. If you're making a beverage, you need one." I laugh.

My mom has none of his assurance. She wrings her hands. She asks what she should do. I am cross-eyed with sleep deprivation; Zoe feeds every two hours. I'm too exhausted to answer.

My mom isn't being the grandma I imagined. I want her to dive in the way she did when my nieces were born. I want her to make bossy declarations like, "New parents need support!" I want her to know more than my brother.

Maybe she's out of sorts because she's in an unfamiliar place. She can't go to the store; she doesn't know where it is. It doesn't help that Zoe is fussy. When she cries, my mom hands her back to me.

She stays on for a few days after my brother leaves. "You are doing too much!" she exclaims, watching me sterilize the breast pump.

"You must have done all this and more," I reply dully. "You had us while you were a doctor."

"That is true."

"I don't know how you did it," I continue. I am drowning just a few days into motherhood. If I can't handle my first couple of weeks, what does that say about me?

My mom came to America when my brother was six months old. It's the only story of motherhood she ever recounts. It was the most difficult period of her life, redoing her residency while dealing with an infant and my father, who, in refusing to change diapers and expecting to have his meals cooked for him, was essentially another child. My mom didn't have the help of a supportive spouse the way I do, plus she had a demanding career in a foreign country.

"Seriously, Mom," I say. "How'd you do it?"

She stops, considers. "I don't know," she answers finally. "I just did." She pats my shoulder. "The same way you will."

Meanwhile, she declares that Zoe has my chin and Noah's fingers, insists that she is unusually alert for a newborn. She is interested in Zoe. This fills something in me. I love hearing her talk to Zoe in Marathi. It makes me soften at her hand-wringing, though with each passing day I wish she could be a little more helpful.

"I'm tired of takeout," she declares one afternoon. "I made a list of things I want from the market."

I look at her in disbelief. Is she really asking me to shop for her?

"If I go to the store, I'll have to leave Zoe with you," I point out.

"Oh." She blinks. "Well, let's just wait for Noah to get home."

I frown at the pots bubbling on the stove that night, spicy fare that will probably give the baby gas. My mom keeps hollering out to ask where things are: the salt, the coriander, the vegetable oil. I grow irritated. Can't she open the cabinets and look?

When she scrubs the cutting board with the baby's bottle-brush—a brush I asked her not to use, a brush I don't want mixing with other things—I explode. "Ugh, Mom! I *specifically told you . . .*" I let the sentence trail off while making a big show of throwing out the brush. At that moment, a cry emanates from the baby monitor. I fly up the stairs, making a mental note to buy a new brush: yet another item on my to-do list.

My mom has always insisted on various "systems" in the kitchen. She of all people should respect my rules. While I know from experience how unpleasant it is to be on the receiving end of her orders, to be reprimanded for cleaning the knife the wrong way, to be lectured on cross-contamination, I take vindictive pleasure in throwing out that brush. I'm the bossy mom now.

When I come down for dinner a little while later, she looks chastised, though a little frazzled. "I'm sorry about the brush," she says, smoothing her hair.

"It's okay," I concede.

I'm about to say more, but Noah throws me a pacifying look. He knows I'll regret it if I do. We eat our meal in silence, waiting for the next little cry from the monitor to sound.

# 11

*M*"*ayudi,* I want to tell you a story," she says.

It is my mother's last night in Seattle. I knocked on her door after Zoe's two A.M. feeding without even the pretense of an excuse. I know that when she leaves, I will miss my mother profoundly. She shushes my apologies, tells me she doesn't mind the late hour, and scoots over on the bed.

"Once, there was a woman in a river—"

"Wait, is this some sort of Indian myth?"

"Hmm. Myth is not quite the right word. Your *agi* told me this story soon after your brother was born. Once, she told me, there was a woman in a river—"

"Is the river the Ganges? Is the woman a goddess, like Lakshmi?"

"I don't remember. You ask so many questions! Do you want me to continue?"

"Yes! I won't interrupt."

"Okay." She clears her throat to ready the tale. "Once, there was a woman in a river. She held a child in her arms—her son. She needed to cross the river. It was much deeper than she expected. As the water reached her chest, she panicked.

"She saw that she had a choice. She could save herself or she could save her child. They would not both make it. What does she do?"

I feel restless, unsure why my mom is telling me the story. "Mom, obviously, she sacrifices herself. That's how all these stories go." Someone gave me a book of Indian illustrated classics when I was young, Hindu myths in comic book form. It was filled with legends of female suffering: Sita swallowed up by the earth; Shakuntala carried up into the heavens. I inhaled those stories, intoxicated by all that feminine virtue.

I can picture the woman in the river: her resigned expression, her last breath before going under, her sari unfurling in a colorful shroud. Logically, the story makes no sense (why would sacrificing herself guarantee her child's safety?), but then, these stories never make sense. The woman's martyrdom is the point. She is beyond logic and beyond reproof. I wonder why my mom has chosen the tale and feel a flicker of annoyance.

My mom chuckles. "That is what I said, too. But that is not what happens."

"She lets her child die?" I say, aghast. "What mom would do that?"

She is silent a long moment before speaking. "What my mother said is that we do not know the outcome. We do not know what the woman will choose. Until we are in the river, up to our shoulders, the current too strong—until we are in that position, we cannot say. We tell ourselves we will sacrifice ourselves for our children, but the will to live is very strong."

I listen, astonished.

"Your *agi* was wise," she continues. "She did not have a lot of education, only through the eighth or ninth grade, but she knew a great deal. We must not judge. This is the lesson of the story. We cannot know the weight of other women's burdens. Whatever a woman decides, it is not easy."

"*Agi* sounds like a feminist," I muse.

"She was, in her own way."

I draw the covers around me. My annoyance with the story has vanished. Something about it comforts me. Maybe it is the surprise of the ending, that the woman choosing herself is even a possibility, or maybe it is the intimacy of my mom talking to me in the middle of the night, just the two of us, the rest of the world asleep. Her whole visit, I wanted her to be helpful. Maybe what I wanted all along was this, the warm focus of her attention. Being cared for, even if that just means being told a story.

I'd expected the woman in the river to sacrifice herself. I realize now the same thing happened with my mom. I'd wanted her to tend to me, and only when she didn't did I see my own expectations—expectations that now shame me. She had flown across the country for me, and I had behaved like a child. Do the demands of motherhood ever cease?

"Being a mom is hard," I finally say.

She murmurs her assent.

We drift off. A couple of hours later, I wake to Zoe's hungry cries. I tiptoe from the room and let my mother sleep.

# 12

After my mom leaves Seattle, I dig up an old photograph of her. My first thought is that she is beautiful. Petite, slender, regal. She has exquisite bone structure: prominent cheekbones, a broad forehead, each feature (her nose, her jaw) distinct, as though carved from fine wood. A long braid runs the length of her spine. She wears an expensive sari, gold bangles at her wrists. Her smile is contained to her mouth. Her eyes are aloof. They know better than to give anything away.

My mom was born in Bombay in 1945. She was born Suhas Sankholkar and became Suhas Shanbhag when she wed, a Brahmin marrying a Brahmin, and though she identifies as a Democrat, she is fiercely proud of her noble caste heritage. She brags about the servants she had on hand throughout her childhood, there to squeeze fresh pomegranate juice or bring her a hot lunch at school, running the whole way to keep it warm. She laughs whenever she recounts this, delighted, while my brother and I wince.

She likes to boast about her grandfather, who stood over six feet tall and had fair skin and green eyes. "Mom, you shouldn't brag about light features," I object. "It makes you sound like some sort of Aryan pride nutjob." "Well," she says, "the word *Aryan* actually comes from Sanskrit. It is true!" She says this possessively, as though wanting credit for the word.

In Marathi, the word for good-looking, *gauri,* is the same as the word for pale. My relatives praised me for how *gauri* I was. "My grandfather's genes," my mom would say proudly.

Physically, I bear no resemblance to her. She is recognizably Indian, while people always try to guess at my heritage with those awful three words: *What are you?* ("Italian?" they ask. "Or, wait, South American?") I am told over and over that I don't look Indian, which is a strange thing to hear. I don't look like what I am.

We are a study in contrasts. Her hair is fine; mine is thick. She is petite and flat-chested; I am taller and curvier. As a girl, I coveted her features. All I wanted was to be *of* her, visibly and identifiably.

Our differences became more apparent when I hit puberty at the unjustly early age of nine. It was like that moment when the Hulk tears through his shirt, an appalling burst of growth. I reached my full height of five-six in the fifth grade. I loomed over my mother.

How I envied her body—the way her button-down blouses sat neatly against her chest while mine gaped in alarm; the elegant compactness of her slim hands and feet while mine flapped gargantuan by contrast. She was orderly and prim: no visible hair on her arms or legs, no need to pluck her perfectly arched brows or tend to the skin above her lip. I never saw her double over with menstrual cramps, never even heard her pass gas. She was a hairless efficient wonder.

It made perfect sense that she was a scientist. She had no need for daydreams. Her body was reliable. Mine betrayed me at every turn.

I used to gaze at her elegantly spare collection of toiletries in the bathroom: a black comb, a silver nail clipper, a single bottle of foundation, CoverGirl in "Golden Tan." The paucity of items spoke to a superiority of being.

I longed for an arsenal of beauty products. I didn't want to enhance my features. I wanted to escape them entirely.

Nothing about my body felt right, but if I could have changed one thing, it would have been my hair. My hair was so thick that plastic headbands spontaneously cracked on my head. My mother refused to brush it, declaring it too much of a hassle. The resulting tangled black nest announced me to the world as different, ethnic. Teachers regarded me with pity.

"Don't get brainwashed," my mom warned when I begged for beauty products. "Those items are a waste of money."

She never wore lipstick or nail polish. She donned slacks and sensible flats to work. The only time I saw her in a dress was at my wedding, and it was a dress I picked out for her after she said imperiously, "I don't have time to for such things. Buy something for me."

Her whole life felt mythic. She was born to an India still under British rule, which struck me as wildly romantic. Even her childhood dog, Ruby, had a thrilling tale. My mom spotted her on a docked ship while accompanying her uncle, a naval inspector, on his rounds. The ship's captain, eager to please the inspector, offered the dog as a gift. Ruby followed my mom home that day, trailing her through the winding streets of Bombay. "Didn't she whine?" I asked. "Didn't you need a leash?" "No," my mom said, "she just followed."

All her stories bear this enchanted quality, dotted with British references: the house on Slater Road; the closest railway stop, Grant Road Station; the private school where she spoke Queen's English and wore a uniform, a white blouse and pleated skirt and patent leather Mary Janes that gave her bunions. Even this flaw struck me as elegant. I used to angle my big toe to try to mimic her tapered feet.

"So you came to the States to give your kids opportunities?" I asked. "Yes," she said, but she wouldn't elaborate.

Adult matters were private. According to Indian custom, women are never to speak their husbands' names aloud. My mom followed this tradition at home. How much information could I expect from her? Her inner life existed behind a wall. On the subject of her childhood, however, she was more forthcoming. She missed India. She and my dad and my brother used to visit every year. My brother even flew there by himself as a kid to spend the summer with my maternal grandparents. By the time I came along, things had changed. My family was more settled in the States.

After her parents died, my mom stopped going back. My dad still traveled to see his family. My mom didn't join him. Without her parents, she saw no reason to return. I stayed behind with her.

She spoke of home wistfully. It became a nostalgic place frozen in time, a butterfly pinned and preserved. She refused to call her birthplace by its new name after it was rechristened Mumbai. It would always be Bombay to her.

An indulged only child, she was given a birthday gift every month by her father. Once a year wasn't enough to celebrate her. She had grown up with a menagerie of pets (doves, lovebirds, squirrels) and never had to lift a finger with so many servants. I had nagging questions (were the servants miserable? wasn't the caste system wrong? what does one feed a squirrel?), but my questions felt petty, intrusive. She didn't want questions. She wanted an audience. I was happy to provide it.

Her wondrous stories gave my childhood color. I listened, rapt, until I could see it: the house on Slater Road, the locomotives at Grant Road Station, a school where children speak Queen's English and, in pleated skirts, twirl and twirl.

# 13

In contrast to my mother's life in India, my childhood home was an unqualified disaster: by turns chaotic, shabby, opulent, dilapidated, spotless.

Imagine if a standard 1970s split-level were owned by a mob boss whose personal style ran to casino grandeur with a touch of Liberace. Then throw in a busy Indian family with a giant incontinent dog. That might sum up the place.

The house was modest, or should have been. The previous owners, with their penchant for glamour, installed a sweeping marble staircase leading up to the front door and swapped the backyard lawn for a white marble patio. The resulting exterior in no way fit the house. It was like pairing a tiara and train with khakis.

Inside, nearly every room had floor-to-ceiling mirrors. My bedroom had a whole wall of mirrors. One of my closet doors was also mirrored. If I opened it and set it at just the right angle, I could see an infinite row of reflections of myself going in either direction. The French term for this is *mise en abyme*. It literally translates to "placed in an abyss."

A hodgepodge of decorative choices: leafy ochre wallpaper in my bedroom, dark brown with silver diamonds in my brother's, blue tile and yellow cabinets in the kitchen, beige tweed on the walls. Powder-blue carpeting throughout. One aqua bathroom.

One orange bathroom. Aquamarine shag carpeting in the basement. A garage of blood red. And then, in case the whole effect was too subtle, there was the chandelier.

Comprised of about two thousand crystals, the entryway chandelier was nearly as large as the staircase. It was my father's contribution to the house. He'd had it shipped to the States from India, an extravagant gesture from an otherwise frugal man. That chandelier belonged in the lobby of a grand hotel. Perhaps a Russian palace. It had no business in a house for reasons of scale and tact. Worse, because you couldn't clean it without leaning perilously over the banister, it remained dusty. The only crystal that got polished with any regularity was at the bottom, a glittering sphere. The rest drooped, opaque and sad.

My parents made no other changes to the house. Dysfunction and discord prevented them doing so. The chandelier is probably still there, a stout dictator too difficult to remove.

I learned basic sterile technique in the kitchen. My mom treated it as a science lab. She flamed utensils that had come into contact with raw meat. She sprayed bleach on the counters. It was spotless.

The rest of the house was not. We didn't walk Fluffy, our Samoyed, nearly enough. He peed and shat his revenge throughout the house, mainly in the basement, the shag carpeting his turquoise turf. He shed massively. Balls of white fur rolled by like tumbleweed. Because we didn't have air-conditioning, he sat miserably in the marble foyer, a polar bear in exile.

In that chaotic space, my childhood task was to locate the scissors when needed. It wasn't simply a hassle to find them. It was impossible. No one ever put them back because there was no "back" for them to go to. The hollered command to find the scissors sent me into a panic that could reduce me to tears. To this day, while my neatness comes and goes, I am tyrannical about the scissors. Opening a drawer and seeing them brings me relief.

That house was an afterthought. It was neglected. No one had time for it. I sympathized. That house was just like me.

I took refuge in stories. Books transported me to farms and ships and castles. Even when bad things happened in novels, the events followed a certain logic. This comforted me.

When my father raged at me for reading, I suspect what he sensed was my disloyalty, that I didn't want to live in his house. He was correct. I wanted out.

# 14

With my mom back in New Jersey and Noah home on a week's paternity leave, we try to settle into a routine. On his last Wednesday before returning to work, I suggest taking Lola and Zoe out for a walk—a prospect I have been dreading.

Lola is a Lab-hound mix of sixty pounds who forgets her training if she catches scent of a squirrel. Zoe is a colicky baby who screams her head off when placed in the stroller. While Noah is untroubled by the prospect of combining the two, I am apprehensive. I can already picture the looks from strangers: *Why can't that woman get her baby to be quiet?* But this is something I need to know I can do.

The day is overcast. As I lower Zoe into the stroller, she whimpers and twists. Lola circles us, her leash getting tangled in the stroller's wheels. It takes ten minutes to get moving, Zoe now wailing. "She'll settle down," Noah promises. A few blocks later, it starts to rain.

Usually in Seattle it "mists." Rarely does it actually rain. This is a downpour. Noah and I fumble for the rain cover, a heap of plastic in the shape of a rhomboid that we turn left and right, up and down, trying to fit it over the stroller. It's like trying to assemble furniture, except in public and with a screaming infant whose comfort depends on your progress. "Forget it!" I yell. I hold the plastic over Zoe's seat with my hands and sprint home.

"It's okay, baby," I holler, feeling so bad for her with each bump and jostle, imagining her wet, cold, miserable. When we get home, she is fast asleep. I'm the one who's wet, cold, and miserable.

Noah bursts into laughter. I burst into tears. "Honey!" he says, alarmed. "What's wrong?" I shake my head, unable to explain it. "I don't think I can do this," I whisper.

I don't know how to describe my feelings, especially because I'm the one who's usually unflappable. He's supposed to be nervous while I reassure *him*.

As a mom, I don't feel permitted to make mistakes. If someone saw Noah fumbling with the rain cover, he'd get sympathy points. *What a great dad!* people would think. It doesn't work this way for moms. If someone saw me, I'd get frowns. *Why would she take her baby out in this weather?* These imagined judgments overwhelm me.

The rest of the day, I feel low. Aware of Noah's impending return to work, I see myself failing in his absence. I am terrified to be on my own. I've heard about local support groups for new moms, but if I can't manage a simple walk, how am I going to handle an unfamiliar drive and a roomful of strangers, all while my baby wails?

The next day, my feelings deepen. It's as though I've been lowered into a well. "Are you okay?" Noah asks. "You don't seem yourself." I stare at him. His words feel distant.

The depths of my gloom hardly make sense to me. Why can't I get a grip? *You're a mom,* I tell myself. *You need to snap out of it.*

By Friday, I am at the bottom of the well. My thoughts are bleak. *I just want to curl up and die,* I keep thinking.

I think I know what this is, but I don't want to face it. The timing is terrible.

"Something's wrong," I finally say. "I want to call my mom, but she's at work."

"Call her," Noah urges. "She'd want you to."

I find the number of Trenton State Hospital and dial with a shaking hand.

"Why are you calling?" she says after getting paged. "I was in a meeting!"

Her voice softens when she hears my sobs.

"I'm sorry, Mom," I choke out. "I didn't mean to bother you. It's just . . . I think I might be depressed."

"Do you have thoughts of harming the baby?" (Her clinical side, calling Zoe "the baby.")

"No."

"Do you have thoughts of harming yourself?"

"Maybe."

She is unfazed. "Do you want to be hospitalized?"

It is a strange relief to be asked this. It means that I am being taken seriously—that I haven't been imagining my symptoms. It also means that I have a say in my own care. "No," I finally answer. "I don't."

"Okay. Good. Get Noah to make an appointment with a psychiatrist. You are going to be fine."

I feel a little better after hanging up, as I always do after calling her. My mom has a proven track record. When she tells me I will be fine, I believe her.

# 15

Noah hits the ground running. He finds a shrink who can see me in a few days, a baby nurse who can start that Sunday.

Usually, I'm the one who drives our decisions. I was the one who found our delivery hospital and pediatrician. I was the one who found our house, our dog. Noah isn't accustomed to taking charge, but he can't consult me now. I am catatonic in bed.

I know that depression isn't a matter of willpower, but I'm furious with myself for my inability to get out of bed. My legs aren't broken. Yet if a fire engulfed the house, I would not budge. It fills me with shame. What kind of a mother am I?

When Noah tells me the cost of the baby nurse, my shame deepens. We will be hemorrhaging money. I am the cause.

"I know you're going to say we can't afford it," Noah says, "but plenty of people hire baby nurses."

I stare at the ceiling.

"We don't have a choice," he continues miserably. "I start work on Monday. I can't leave you by yourself. Not when you're like this."

I hear the plea in his voice. He wants me to forgive him for getting help. He wants me to be back in charge.

# 16

Caren is from Trinidad. She arrives at the door in nursing scrubs, a consummate professional. I see the living room through her eyes: piles of diaper boxes, burp cloths strewn across surfaces. It isn't exactly the first impression I want to make, but I'm too tired to care.

She runs through how she likes to do things: a feeding chart, a sleep chart, a bedtime ritual. "We want to get the baby on a schedule," she explains.

"A schedule?" I repeat. I haven't been able to get Zoe to sleep for more than thirty minutes at a stretch. Caren might as well offer to broker peace in the Middle East.

"Absolutely, Mom." She refers to me and Noah as "Mom" and "Dad," which is disconcerting but nice. Zoe can't yet say the words. Maybe I need to hear them.

"Look," I stammer, "I'm not sure what Noah said about how long you'd be with us, but I'm hoping to get better pretty fast."

"I know. I get it."

"But you need to know how long you'll be here, right? That's only fair to you."

"Don't worry about me. I hear you've been on your own this whole time. Postpartum depression. Colic. It's a lot. You should rest."

"Oh. Well, I was going to show you where everything is—

Zoe's room, the bottles. And, God, I haven't offered you anything. Would you like some tea?"

She smiles. "Relax, Mom. I can take care of myself."

"How will you know where to find things?"

"Because this is what I do."

I don't think I'll be able to trust a stranger with my child, but Caren earns that trust. She rubs Zoe's back in circles rather than pat, which helps with her acid reflux. She sets the crib mattress at a thirty-degree angle, which helps Zoe sleep. She sings funny made-up songs. Soon, I find myself growing drowsy.

"Rest, Mom," Caren says, swaddling Zoe. "I've got this."

The words are a gift.

# 17

The next day I see a shrink, a patrician man with white hair and a discreetly tucked away hearing aid. His office is elegant. Freud lines the bookshelves, the same blue Strachey editions I once studied in grad school. A lifetime ago, it seems.

"I'm glad you were able to get help so quickly," he observes. "How did you recognize this as depression?"

"I was depressed once before, in college. And my mom is a psychiatrist."

He nods and takes notes.

After the appointment, I call my mom to tell her about it. All she wants to know is which antidepressant I've been prescribed. "*What?*" she says, outraged, when I read out the name and dosage. "Tear up the script! I will call in a new one. My way is better."

I don't doubt it.

"Give me this man's number," she continues. "He should not make the same mistake with his other patients."

"Do you think I shouldn't see him? That he isn't any good?"

"Not at all. He just doesn't have my expertise. He may be useful in other capacities."

"Like what?"

"Well, it's important that you're under someone's supervision. And talking to someone can be helpful . . . for additional and supplementary support." She speaks these last words as though reading them from a pamphlet.

The main thing, she says, is to hang in there until the medication kicks in. Depression is a broken bone no one can see. She explained this time and time again when I was a kid. Therapy is an ice pack for the swelling. It might offer some relief, but it does nothing for the underlying fracture.

"I'd like to think I'm more than just an ice pack," my shrink says at our next session. He wants to see me twice a week until I start to feel better.

"Twice a week!" I say, alarmed.

"Probably he just wants extra money," says my mom.

# 18

A week later I'm doing all the right things—seeing the shrink, taking medication, going for a daily walk—but none of it is helping.

Basic tasks (getting out of bed, brushing my teeth) require superhuman strength. It feels like I'm wading through a pool of black tar with a hundred-pound backpack saddling my shoulders. Glancing at the clock causes desperation. How can it only be five minutes from when I last looked? If this is how the minutes pass, how will I get through a whole day?

Zoe cries incessantly. Hearing of an epic seventeen-hour crying fit, the pediatrician tells me it's one of the worst cases of colic she's encountered. She asks if I have enough support. I recoil from the question. I hear it as an accusation.

*She can tell you aren't cut out for this,* says a snide little voice in my head. *It's obvious to everyone.*

The voice has been popping up in my thoughts. It's a demonic voice that undercuts me. It sees right through me.

One night when Caren is away, I wake up to the sound of Zoe's cries, more piercing than usual. I rush to her and find Noah standing over her crib, his hands on his head. "Why can't you just sleep?" he hollers. I usher him out of the room and take Zoe in my arms, rocking her.

*See?* the voice sneers. *You're not really depressed. If you were really depressed, you'd kill yourself. Faker!*

Each blessing in my life looks like a burden. My beautiful baby? My caring husband? All I can think about is how much better off they would be without me.

While I recognize that my thoughts are distorted, I can't regain perspective. Then I feel even more worthless. I am trapped in an endless negative loop.

The demonic voice reminds me that there is only one way out. It taunts me for how much money I'm costing my family. It lambastes me for feeling sorry for myself when other people have it so much worse. It whispers that I am a waste of space. Noah and Zoe will be happier without me. They will be free of the nuisance I have become.

I should stop trying to wade through the black muck. I should close my eyes and just give in. Things would be so much easier that way.

I look at my daughter and feel guilty for not enjoying her.

I look at my husband and feel terrible for burdening him.

I look at the gray sky and feel utterly alone.

# 19

Because I can't banish the voice, because I don't know how much more I can take, I call my mom. "I'm sorry to bother you," I say, fighting tears. "I know you're busy. It's just . . . life doesn't feel worth living anymore."

"Please don't say that, *Mayudi.*"

"Mom." I summon my courage, tell myself to say the thing I've been trying so hard not to say. "I need you. I know it's not convenient right now, that you were just here, but it would help so much to see you. Even if it's just for the weekend—"

"I wish I could."

I stare out the window at the neighbor's tall cedar, brown and green, surrounded by an expanse of gray. "The thing is, you *can.* You're acting like you can't, but I could buy you a plane ticket. You could leave on Friday after work. You could come for the weekend."

The line goes quiet.

"I—I wouldn't ask unless I needed it," I continue. "I know I have Caren. And the shrink. So much support, right? It should be enough. But the thing is, I've been thinking about . . . you know . . . ending it. I don't think I can take it anymore."

She is supposed to have interrupted by now. She is supposed to say, *Of course,* Mayudi. *Have Noah buy the ticket.* These are the words I desperately want to hear.

"Mom? Listen, I know you've been tired—"

"If I could be there I would," she says suddenly. "I can't. You must accept this."

"But . . . isn't this more important than work? What could be more important than this? I don't understand."

"If I tried to come to you right now I would die on the plane. And would that make you feel any better? No."

I take the phone from my ear and stare at it. "Is this some sort of joke?"

"Joke? Why would I joke?"

"You're saying you would *die*? Of what?"

"Exhaustion! My body cannot handle travel anymore. The last thing you need is a dead mother. That would not help your situation, believe me."

My mother is countering my death claim with one of her own. I can't believe it.

"What mom reacts this way? You're being ridiculous! You wouldn't die on the plane. Who dies on a plane? But people with depression commit suicide all the time. If that happened, how would you feel?"

I listen to myself trying to persuade her of my worth. I want to build my case, tell her exactly how I'd do it, ask how she'd feel at my funeral, but all I hear is my desperation. She already said no. How much more do I want to humiliate myself? Besides, wouldn't it be better if I just went ahead and did it?

I picture the scene, graffiti on the walls, *if only you had come* splashed in black, her remorse hitting her like a brick. The demonic voice cheers this vision, thrilled that I am finally catching on. *We are all alone in this world,* the voice says. *See?*

"She must not have understood how bad things are," says Noah when he comes home from work.

"Yeah, well, I made it pretty clear."

He calls her later that night. He hangs up ten minutes later looking stunned. Her position didn't change. It never does.

# 20

That afternoon, I am devastated. My devastation swallows me. The situation is too implausible to comprehend.

My whole life, I believed my mom would be there for me. I took it on faith that if I needed her, she would appear. She was my backup parachute. Now that I've finally pulled the cord, I've found it attached to nothing.

Part of me wants to make good on my threat out of spite. I want to explode her world with grief. *My daughter needed me and I didn't come.* I want her to speak those words—but if I am gone, I won't hear them.

That afternoon, I am at a juncture. I can listen to the demonic voice or I can reject it. I can see the world as a place where I am alone or I can look past my mother's reaction. I can suffer or I can ask for help.

Just beyond these walls, I have support. I am not alone. "You know, I'm not just here for the baby. I'm here for you," Caren sometimes says softly. I haven't really leaned on her. I haven't really leaned on anyone. I've been too scared. But the demonic voice wants me to feel that way. It counts on my silence.

I look around at the room I am in: the gray sky, the closed door. I can stay in this room or I can be brave. I reach for the doorknob without wiping my tears.

# 21

Caren consoles me, her hand flying up to her mouth in shock when she hears the story. The shrink calls back within minutes of my leaving him a voicemail. "It's lucky you checked your messages when you did," I remark. "Lucky?" he repeats. "I've been checking nonstop out of concern for you!"

Caren and the shrink are furious on my behalf, as is Noah. I don't interrupt when they express their indignation. I don't defend my mother. I let their words sink in.

A funny thing happens. A small red balloon forms inside me. I feel it deep in my chest. It grows as Noah and Caren and the shrink voice their fury.

The red balloon is anger. I've never let myself be angry before. I didn't want to be like my dad. Giving in to my anger doesn't cripple me, though. It lifts me. The red balloon helps me rise.

My life comes into focus with new clarity.

I won't mope. I won't let my mother's reaction defeat me. I won't let anyone have that kind of power over me, not even my mom.

# 22

The drugs kick in a week later, about two weeks after starting them.

One morning I wake up feeling normal. *Oh,* I think. *I'm back.* The difference is as clear as having power restored after a storm.

Getting out of bed isn't a chore.

The demonic voice is gone.

I race to the crib to see Zoe.

I stroke her hair, touch her cheek, feel all the things I am supposed to feel. My eyes fill with tears. The good kind.

# 23

I am lucky to beat the depression. Most people wouldn't be able to afford a baby nurse or a shrink. Most people don't have such a supportive spouse. I repeat these facts over and over to lessen my ache over my mother.

The red balloon has since deflated. My anger, so powerful, has fled. It was easy to be outraged at my mom when I was drowning. Now that I've washed up on shore, I feel a numb awareness of what transpired.

A host of emotions register—pain, betrayal, confusion. Mostly, though, I am embarrassed. I made it. I'm okay, just as my mom predicted.

Wasn't it a little melodramatic of me to ask her to fly across the country? Who was I to be so demanding?

When she immigrated to the States, my brother an infant, she must have missed her parents terribly. She managed. She didn't have help.

Motherhood has proved harder, more exhausting, than anything I've done before. I have so much I want to say about it. Then I remember my mom's stoicism. Sleep deprivation, breast-feeding: to her they required no comment.

I want to be as strong as she was. I want my story of motherhood to be every bit as heroic, not filled with these embarrassments (a baby nurse! a shrink!) but one of self-sufficiency.

# 24

***

As the weeks pass, Caren long gone, Zoe sweeter than ever, I pretend the phone call never happened. It's easy enough to do. My mom is delighted to hear about Zoe's latest adorable feat. Who else can I talk to about tummy time?

*You were suicidal and she refused to visit.* The thought surfaces at odd moments: while folding laundry or doing dishes, the pristine new bottle brush on the counter. I turn away from it. "Hi, Mom!" I chirp when she picks up the phone.

"Do you really expect to move on without acknowledging this?" the shrink asks.

I have mixed feelings about seeing him. Though it is a relief to confide in someone, I'm embarrassed by my ongoing need for support. Now that the depression is behind me, I want this to be the happiest time of my life. By some miracle, the sessions are covered by insurance, so I go for the silliest of reasons: It's free.

"You confessed to suicidal ideation!" he says. "Her reaction would wound anyone."

Maybe, or maybe my mom was actually being a brilliant psychiatrist. Maybe she knew from years of experience that I wasn't a serious threat to myself, even as I insisted, very seriously, that I was. She knew there would be no benefit to coddling me.

"Coddling?" the shrink repeats. "Do you truly view getting help this way?"

I suppose I do.

"Her reaction doesn't strike you as odd? Her words about dying on the plane?"

That part, I have to admit, is strange. "The thing is," I counter, "if she'd hesitated that day on the phone, if she'd waffled, I think it would have been harder for me. She was so certain. So adamant! Her refusal to back down . . . it goaded me into anger. And in a strange way, that helped."

"How so?"

"Anger was a nice change from the depression. It was, I don't know, energizing."

"You're saying this was deliberate on her part? If so, she was taking quite the risk."

I think back to that day on the phone: the gray sky, the neighbor's cedar. I will never know what went through my mom's head, but I know my threats weren't idle.

"You bend over backward to defend your mother. Have you thought about discussing your feelings with her?"

I look away. The shrink doesn't understand. I can't afford to confront my mom. Even as a teenager, I avoided fights with her. "My parents are divorced," I tell people, "but my mom and I are *really, really close.*" She's the only parent I have. It's not a relationship I'm willing to risk.

# 25

It is a cruel feature of memory that trauma retains its vividness while love fades to a blur. I don't have too many recollections of my mom from early childhood, but the ones of my dad are clear.

Seven years old, summer. He sends me to the driveway because he finds a crayon of mine under the couch.

He orders me to stand barefoot on the blacktop. He will watch me from the living room window to make sure I don't hop between feet or go on the grass.

The blacktop shimmers, nearly liquid under the July sun. I cry, my feet as hot as my shame. I tell myself to move but can't.

A police car drives by, a rarity on our suburban street. I think about flagging the car down for help but worry I will get my family in trouble.

Later, the shock of cool water. A yellow basin. My mother's hands at my blistered feet.

She takes me to Friendly's for ice cream. I order the Reese's sundae. I don't like its sticky sweetness, but I like her concern. "Please eat, *Mayudi*," she says softly. Finishing the sundae will show her that I am okay. I eat it dutifully, spoon by spoon.

Eight years old. Mrs. Greenfield's class. The blackboard is a friendly green she fills with white chalk. Sunlight spills across my desk.

I get a hundred and four on the first spelling quiz. "I thought at first you had a ninety-nine, which is why I wrote that," Mrs. Greenfield says. "Then I saw that you'd put the extra credit on the back, and you got all five of those very hard words right! So I changed your score."

I look at the quiz: a red 99 with a single line through it, then the 104 with an exclamation point for good measure. Feeling brave, I ask my dad to sign it. Mrs. Greenfield's classroom, the way she looks at me, that definitive exclamation point—all of these suggest hope.

He studies the quiz. He studies me. Mom would have signed by now.

"Do you think I am a fool?" he roars. "Crossing out the ninety-nine! As if a teacher would make such a dumb mistake! Anyone can see the hundred and four is in different handwriting. You should be ashamed! Cheating like this!" Without warning, his hand flies out and catches my cheek. I touch my skin, stunned.

I burst into tears, but my feelings aren't directed at him. I'm angry with myself for not knowing better.

When Mrs. Greenfield asks why the quiz is unsigned, I say that I forgot. Something—a quaver in my voice, the look in my eyes—causes her to sigh rather than make me bring it home again. For this, I am grateful.


Nine years old. Words open a door. I've always loved to read, but writing is a new form of magic. I can fashion my own escape hatch.

I write a series of poems about the idea of nothing: what happens when we turn off the lights, what exists in an empty room, the fact that "nothing" is a word and therefore *something*. I spend a Saturday afternoon copying the poems out in my best handwriting. I tack them to my wall, rearranging them until the sequence is just right.

Because the only books in our house are my parents' medical and engineering textbooks, I don't know that writing a series on a topic is the norm among poets. I think I have discovered the concept. I think I am a *genius*.

My father enters my room. He studies the poems while I watch from the bed. He removes one and tears it to pieces.

"Take all this down. What a waste! When I was your age . . ."

I can tell he's getting wound up. He makes himself angrier as he talks, the original offense doubling and tripling in his mind, the problem no longer the poems but the larger issue, which is me. Soon he is throwing invectives. "Stupid girl!" "Irresponsible girl!" "Spoiled American girl!"

I take deep breaths. It's my constant resolution: *Don't cry. Not this time.*

"What do you think these are? Poems?" He sneers the word. "You think you are, what, an artist? A *writer*?"

Later, when I'm older, a friend tells me about a childhood incident when he was bullied and called a fag. Though he registered the intended insult, he also felt a pang of recognition, a "Wait! So that's what I am?"

It's what happens to me that day. I'm used to my father firing insults at me—"worthless girl" is the one that usually gets me sobbing—but that afternoon, the word *writer* is an arrow hitting an altogether different target. Writer! I can't believe there's a word for what I am. I sit up straighter inside.

Though I take down the poems as ordered, though I put them in the trash rather than hide them (he will only find them and yell at me), it is worth it, to have heard that word. That day, for once, I don't cry.

# 26

He was an engineer. He had a moustache and bottle-thick glasses. He wrote in block letters. He was absent-minded.

Often while driving, something would catch his eye and he'd look off, head turned one way, the car going another. We got into more than one accident this way. After I received my driver's license, he told me the best way to switch lanes isn't to check your blind spot. It's to begin merging and see if anyone honks.

He liked when things were black and white. He disliked when things didn't make sense to him. He was color-blind, a trait that suited him perfectly. He couldn't see nuance.

In middle school, when I made the track team as a sprinter, he took me to the local track after he came home from work. "Again!" he would shout, making me race him over and over. "I am fifty, an old man! You should be able to beat me!" Between team practice and these evening sessions, I developed shin splints. My dad told me to run through them. My shins became so inflamed I couldn't put on pants without crying. The pediatrician diagnosed stress fractures. I quit track.

A year later when I made the tennis team, he took me to the local courts and screamed at me to get each ball after the first bounce. People gawked. "Sir," intervened a woman in a visor, "it's not right for you to yell at your daughter like that. It's *just not right*." She smiled at me. I shrank. I felt humiliated by her concern. I knew my father would only yell at me more once we were out of sight.

If only I were stronger, he wouldn't need to yell. I knew he was trying to toughen me up. As he explained, I should be grateful.

His words made logical sense to me. I *should* ignore my own exhaustion. I *should* wake up at seven A.M. in the summer to clean the house. I *should* be gracious to guests and serve them food. These felt like reasonable points for self-improvement.

If only I could listen. If only I could be less needy. As is, I was all wrong. I was wrong in my appearance, wrong in my choices, wrong in my thinking, wrong in my body. If a child is a story in progress, he wanted to rewrite me. His alternate version was appealing, as seductive as the stories from my Indian comic book.

# 27

"One day, I will divorce him," my mom would promise. It was my deepest wish as a kid, what I secretly hoped for every year at Christmas. My dad yelled. My mom was gentle. It was no contest. I wanted to be with her.

Sometimes she made the promise at Friendly's, ice cream our coping ritual for his temper. Or she would say it after seeing evidence of his latest outburst. "What happened to the clock?" she'd ask, picking it up from the floor. Then she'd look at me. "Oh."

With each year, I believed her less. "There are things you don't understand," she'd mutter. "I must wait until you are older to leave him. Children of divorce have a terrible time. I see it all the time in my work." Her justifications vexed me. If she were staying for my sake, why tell me? Sharing her plan of divorce didn't protect me from the concept.

However flawed her logic, I was glad she talked with me. Had she pretended her marriage was fine, had she ignored his behavior, it would have been worse. Acknowledging the situation validated my perceptions. It meant that the tensions in our home weren't my fault. They couldn't be if she had trouble with him, too.

"People with problems can't be there for their children," she sometimes told me. She was referring to her patients, the schizophrenics and addicts, but she held my gaze for an extra beat. *Your father is one such person.* She never spoke the words, but I felt them.

I existed at the cusp of her perceptions, at the limit of what she was willing to acknowledge. It was as though she were laying out an equation. He was unstable. She wanted to leave him but couldn't. I was the reason why—the variable.

I wasn't sure how to solve the problem, but I saw a fundamental choice with parenthood, the terms of the equation itself. You could be the parent who devotes herself to her children, or you could be the source of instability. You could offer unconditional love, or you could be a pit of need. You could be like her, or you could be like him.

# 28

I don't usually talk about my father. I never thought I deserved to. I was provided for financially. I went to excellent schools. Who was I to complain?

I reminded myself that other kids have it worse. I thought about children whose parents molest them or abandon them in the name of alcohol or drugs. Doing so never made me feel better. That abuse happens in horrific forms and with all too much frequency does not normalize it. Contemplating worse pain didn't lessen mine.

Whenever I saw girls with caring fathers, something in me went cold. My dad never hugged me. He never said he loved me. I didn't know how that felt. To be accepted by my dad was already a stretch. Being adored—I couldn't fathom it.

All I knew was that he had specific rules of conduct for me, rules I only became aware of after breaking them: standing the wrong way at the Hindu temple, wearing outfits that were too revealing, reading filth from the library, revering pop culture when I should be serious.

I should never be late when meeting someone; girls don't keep people waiting. I should never complain about physical discomfort; I had a good life. I should never primp or preen (which was conceited), wear makeup (which was slutty), or dance (which sent the wrong message).

After my parents' divorce, my dad fell out of my life. His way of seeing me had been through my mom. I felt better not seeing him, but this confused me. Shouldn't I want him in my life? Shouldn't he want to be in *mine*? Whenever he called, my guilt caused me to pretend everything was fine, no matter if it had been months since we last spoke.

Years later when I moved to New York, we met a few times for dinner. The meals were awkward affairs. He went on at length about his job and his co-workers, tensions with them, while I listened and nodded. He didn't ask about my life. Afterward, I felt agitated, nagged by a sense that this wasn't how children and parents were supposed to interact. The meals felt more like bad dates.

I was relieved in moving to Seattle to put some distance between us. His lack of interest in my life was easier to bear from three thousand miles away. It wasn't until after Zoe was born, however, that I was able to banish my guilt.

How my father rates on the spectrum of awfulness no longer interests me. I used to be in a defensive posture where he was concerned. I justified his behavior by telling myself it wasn't that bad. I kept quiet not because he was awful, but because to my mind he wasn't awful *enough*.

It feels good to come out of that crouch. It feels good to stand up and stretch and say what happened, not because I require anything of the listener, but for the simple pleasure of standing tall.

# 29

The days grow longer and lighter. I am smitten with Zoe. At three months old, she babbles and smiles, loves her bath, and is the happiest of babies now that her colic is gone. She isn't sleeping through the night, isn't sleeping much at all, actually, but I'm managing. I'm even working on a novel, one that has been in my thoughts for some time.

I always dismissed the idea of writing a novel, because doing so felt foolish, outlandish, a pipe dream. Zoe makes me look at dreams anew. Aren't dreams rather wonderful? How can I urge her to pursue hers if I don't pursue mine?

I once hoped my daughter would distract me from the question of what to do with my life. Instead, she holds up a mirror. I see that I've been running from my dreams. My whole life, I've been doing it. When I was pre-med, when I was a management consultant and then an academic, I knew those paths weren't right for me. I sought to be impressive because I was scared to face my desires.

The voice that mocks me for wanting to write is a cousin of depression's demonic voice. *What do you think you are, an artist? A writer?* I know that voice. I've spent too much of my life listening to it.

I decide to give my novel a shot, even though I am exhausted and sleep-deprived, my thoughts cobwebbed. I'm hardly my sharpest, but at least I'm motivated.

As Zoe absorbs her world, I see that I anchor it. It's sobering. If I want the voice in her head to be one of encouragement, I have to give that gift to myself. By taking care of myself, I am taking care of her.

The whole thing makes me rethink motherhood. At awards ceremonies, someone always tearfully acknowledges their mother. "She sacrificed everything for me," the person says, breaking down. I don't want Zoe going through life thinking that I gave myself up for her. I don't want guilt to be her inheritance.

My assumptions of motherhood have been all wrong. I feared I was supposed to have all the answers. I didn't know my daughter would help me find them. I worried she would be an obstacle to my dreams, not the reason I went after them. Zoe makes me want to be the best version of myself. That isn't sacrifice. It's inspiration.

And so, after Noah comes home from work, after making dinner and putting Zoe to bed, I go to a late-night coffee shop. It isn't easy. I feel guilty for leaving. Having been up since dawn, I get tempted by the couch, wanting nothing more than to curl up and watch bad TV. But once I am at the café, once I am at my usual table with nothing but my own thoughts, it is bliss.

New moms are told to take care of ourselves, to get a massage or have a glass of wine with girlfriends. Those things don't do it for me. The idea of a massage makes me wince at the cost. Any girlfriends in Seattle are new; we're still in the audition stages of friendship. Only in my writing am I able to let go.

It sounds like the worst time to weigh one's desires, as a new parent, but maybe it's the best, the most necessary. When tasked with caring for a human being, when asked to subsume one's own needs, this is when we require a firmer grasp on ourselves. Rather than telling new moms to indulge, to do the frivolous activities women in movies do, we should say this: Find yourself. Gather yourself up before it is too late. You are at risk of getting buried. Maybe you're already feeling buried. Do something that will solidify your sense of self, buttress your retaining walls. Don't worry if it feels scary. It's probably a good thing if it does.

Working on my novel for an hour or two restores me. I return home from the coffee shop feeling renewed.

Perhaps this is what we should give new moms: A laptop and a cup of coffee. A notebook and a pen. Permission to dream.

# 30

That spring, when Zoe is four months old, I hear from my dad.

He didn't call when Zoe was born. He never knew my due date. His only way of acknowledging the arrival of his granddaughter was to send me a belated one-line email congratulating me on "Zeo." None of that surprised me.

His latest missive, like everything from him, comes out of the blue. He is engaged to be married, he writes. A long paragraph ensues about his fiancée. They plan to visit Seattle and stay with me for a week. What dates look good?

I close my laptop. I reopen it a second later to ensure I haven't hallucinated. A shaky feeling comes over me. It's the same jittery feeling I get whenever my dad resurfaces in my life.

I forward the message to Noah and to a close friend. Misery shared is misery lessened. I walk around the rest of the day feeling skittish.

I have no idea how to reply. I haven't seen my dad in two years. The prospect of him showing up at my house with a woman I've never met . . . it's unthinkable.

Yet I know exactly what he pictures. He will expect me to cook and clean and play hostess. It doesn't occur to him that I might not want to see him. Hearing from him is disconcerting for this reason. I'm supposed to drop everything for him.

I am a character in a story my father tells, that he is a success-ful man with a good family. It doesn't matter to him if the story doesn't match reality. It doesn't matter to him if it isn't true. He expects me to reflect well on him.

Years earlier, when my brother got married, my dad threw a party. He invited his friends and certain relatives. He put on a slideshow of photographs, including recent pictures of my mom. Certain guests didn't know about the divorce. The slideshow painted a rosy portrait of a family still intact. "So where is your mother?" people asked politely. "Was she not feeling well today?"

Everyone urges me to refuse my father's visit. "This is the last thing you need," says Noah. "You haven't seen him in years! He can't just waltz into your house with his lady friend!" my friend says angrily. "Tell Dad you're busy," suggests my brother.

I know they're right, but I've never said no before. Whenever my dad calls, I comply.

Despite the advice pouring in from all sides, it is wordless Zoe who makes me rethink the situation. She prompts me to think about good parents instead of good daughters. I don't want her to feel obligated to anyone, especially if it compro-mises her well-being. If that applies to her, it must apply to me.

I write back and tell my dad it isn't a great time. I expect to feel guilty, like a terrible human being. Instead, I feel relief. For once, I've made my life easier. I've been my own ally, just as I want Zoe to be for herself. I'm making better choices in my life not despite my child, but because of her.

I'm prepared for ramifications, but my dad doesn't write back. He doesn't call. Weeks later, his fiancée leaves him. He doesn't offer to visit without her.

That email is the last exchange we ever have.

# 31

I contemplate ending my sessions with the shrink. I've finally stood up for myself with my dad. I'm no longer taking the antidepressant. I'm even writing a novel! Surely these are positive developments.

What draws me back to his office is the subject of my mom. The shrink seems intent on getting me to view her in a different light. It feels like he's trying to take her away from me. This can't be the case. I decide to bring the issue front and center.

"This being psychoanalysis, everything has to be my mom's fault, right?" I joke. "But it sounds like you want to blame her for my depression."

"Is the idea so outlandish?"

I stare at him. "You . . . you were supposed to contradict me."

"You don't see any connection between her actions and your illness?"

He can't be serious. My eyes rake his walls for diplomas. Did the man even go to medical school? "Depression isn't caused by mommy issues. It's caused by dips in neurotransmitters."

"Yes, but we don't know what causes those dips. Circumstances play a part."

"I'd just given birth! The changes in hormones were responsible."

"You don't see any other contributing factors?"

"Factors like what?" I ask, bewildered.

"Like the absence of support! Women who don't feel supported going into labor are more likely to experience depression."

"No, no, no." I shake my head. "That stuff applies to single moms, or, I don't know, women who don't have caring partners. Not to me."

"You describe your mother as always being there for you—"

"Because she *was*."

"I have a hard time believing her refusal to visit came out of nowhere. You are determined to give her credit I am not sure she has earned."

Hearing this is like being slapped.

"Tell me," he says gently, "did her behavior change recently? Was there any indication that she wouldn't be there for you?"

I think about how she quit her job. I think about how she declared herself old. I think about how I don't want him to be right. I set my jaw. "Nope."

"Did you miss her while pregnant?"

"No!" I nearly shout. I catch myself on the edge of my chair, my hands clenched. I force my body to relax. "I mean, okay, maybe a *little*," I concede, "but there have been plenty of other times I missed her. I wasn't depressed then."

"What other times?"

"Well, like when I went to boarding school—"

"You went to boarding school?" He jots a note in his pad.

"Yeah, but it was my choice!" I try to read his writing upside down. "The point is, I wasn't depressed!"

He takes a different tack. "When you *were* depressed in college, how did she respond then?"

"How did she *respond*?" I repeat sarcastically. "She helped me! She was the reason I got better!"

But as I say this, a memory creeps into my thoughts: freshman year, lying in bed in my dorm room for days, perhaps weeks, my friends and boyfriend concerned because I won't get up, not even to go to class. My mom plans to take me to see a doctor over winter break. They want me to go to the medical center right away. I am too ashamed, a shame that has to do with the fact that fancy college resources cannot possibly be for me.

I should have known better, but my mom should have, too. If it were Zoe, would I let her suffer like that?

The shrink regards me, waiting for me to speak.

"I just . . . I don't understand why you keep bringing her up," I finally say. "I want to move *forward*."

"You don't think your past is relevant?"

"Look, I was an English major. I know what I'm supposed to say. 'The past isn't even the past,' right? But that's literature. This is my life."

He regards me over his glasses.

"I know what you're thinking," I add. "You're thinking I'm resisting you on the subject of my mom. It's what Freud would say. But the problem with Freud is that there's no room for disagreement. If a patient resists, she's in denial. And this *isn't* denial!"

He nods, but I swear his mouth twitches.

"You said boarding school was your choice," he says. "Tell me about that."

# 32

What I tell casual acquaintances: The public school in my town had a series of budget cuts. Boarding school seemed like a good idea because I wanted to be challenged academically. "Makes sense," people respond.

What I tell friends: I fantasized about boarding school as a kid (who doesn't?) and convinced my mom to send me by telling her that my public school was going downhill. I made her see *Dead Poets Society* as part of my campaign. The public school hadn't really suffered. The lie was my ticket out.

What really happened is something I've never told a soul. I kept the truth hidden, as did my parents.

I pictured the different versions of the story (false, somewhat true, completely true) like rings on a dartboard. There was the outer zone for acquaintances, the inner ring for friends, but no one was ever to see the bull's-eye. I could let people in closer, but always through carefully calibrated stories that made me into someone relatable and normal, away from the red danger zone. What really happened was something my parents and I skirted until it felt like it had never happened at all.

# 33

What really happened is this. When I was thirteen, I tried to kill myself.

My father was watching a movie one afternoon in the living room. I walked in on a scene where a prisoner slit his wrists. I wasn't frightened. I felt a thrill of possibility. I never knew taking your life was an option. It was like discovering a new page on a menu.

Usually, I went to bed at night hoping to die. I wanted to be one of those kids who perished from a rare cancer. I didn't want pity. I wanted out. What other solution was there to the problem of my dad?

The Internet didn't exist back then. I couldn't look up how to do it properly. I studied my wrists. I figured a vertical cut was probably better than a horizontal one, like opening a string bean. I decided to do it on a Monday, when my mom worked late.

The mirrored door of my bedroom closet had an intricate carved design, part of which was damaged. A sharp edge had once sliced open my thumb. I rubbed my wrist against it. Nothing. I brought it down at an angle. No good.

I took a paring knife from the kitchen. Right hand. Left wrist. I must have missed the vein or not cut deeply enough. I switched hands. My left hand was dexterous from years of playing the piano. I aimed directly at a blue vein.

There was blood, but not enough—nothing like the dramatic spurt in the movie. Bandaging myself up, I figured I'd try again later.

That night, my dad stormed into my room and started yelling at me. It was how most Monday nights went. My outfits were too revealing, he said. Walking around in tight pants! I should be ashamed!

I took my usual calming breaths. I told myself not to cry.

"Worthless girl! Bringing attention to your body. You want to be a slut?"

The futility of trying not to cry. The betrayal of my tear ducts. The feeling that there was no escaping him.

He left the room and came back with scissors. Even in that moment of fear, some part of me wondered how he'd located them so fast. He yanked my leggings from the drawer and started hacking at them.

"Stop!" I finally cried, for he was about to slash my silver leggings, the only ones that were remotely cool. "You can't do this! It isn't right!"

"Right?" he sneered. "Who are you to tell me what's right?"

"Because of this!" I held up my bandaged wrists. "When you yell at me, it makes me do this!"

His eyes bulged, not from anger this time, but from shock. When he lowered the scissors, it felt like victory. "You—you cut yourself?" he said.

"I tried to kill myself," I answered defiantly.

He left the room.

I knew I was in trouble. He'd tell my mom when she got home. God only knew what would happen then.

I listened for her car in the driveway that night, but I didn't run downstairs like usual. I pretended to be asleep. My father opened the garage for her. I heard them talking in low murmurs. I couldn't sleep that night, uncertain of my fate. I told myself that at least there would be no more secrets, no more pretending that everything was okay. I'd given my parents something even they couldn't ignore.

The next morning, my mom didn't say a word on the drive to school. She picked me up at the end of the day, only she didn't go back to work. She stayed home that afternoon.

I practiced piano. She came and sat beside me on the bench. I kept playing, my eyes on the sheet music, my heart beating wildly.

"Your father," she said.

My fingers paused on the keys.

"Your father said you tried to hurt yourself?"

I said nothing.

"Can I see?"

I lifted my sleeves. She glanced at the bandages.

"Don't ever do that again, okay?"

I hesitated. "Okay."

I resumed playing, shakily at first. After a while, the notes came smoothly. It was a relief. I had always disliked the way my mom swept things under the rug, but now I saw the wisdom of her approach. I was glad she didn't make a big fuss. I preferred the cover story that I was fine.

A week later, I brought up the idea of boarding school. I didn't mention needing to get away from my dad. In my most grown-up voice, I said, "You know how public schools are getting these days." She nodded thoughtfully.

*Dead Poets Society* features an artsy teenager who commits suicide because of a controlling father. We didn't say anything about that, either.

"Not too far away." These were her only instructions for me.

I went to the library, asked the librarian about boarding

schools "not too far," and applied to the two schools she off-handedly mentioned.

I had finally solved the problem, the equation my mother had presented so long ago. The answer was to remove the variable. The answer was to get rid of me.

Soon after, I heard my mom talking at a dinner party. "These public schools!" she said. "They are going downhill!"

All these years later, I still have a faint scar on my right wrist, a bit of skin on the cusp of a vein that sometimes catches the light, satiny. I'm glad for it. It's the only proof I have of what happened, a ghost of the truth that goes unsaid.

# 34

At my final session with the shrink, I am given pause by how sad he looks.

"I'm better," I point out. "No longer depressed!"

"Yes," he says heavily, "but the conditions that contributed to your depression—though you don't see it that way—concern me. I worry about the situation with your mother, to be frank."

"Why?"

"Because these issues will resurface."

His words haunt me. Upon hearing the real story of why I went to boarding school, he viewed it a little differently than I did. While I saw a mom who knew better than to get bent out of shape, he saw a pattern of neglect. "Neglect!" I sputtered.

My mom is thrilled when I stop seeing him. "He was a quack!" she says happily.

"He thought I should continue the sessions."

"Of course he thought that. You were a good source of revenue."

"Mom . . . he wanted me to talk with you about, well, how you didn't visit."

"Only because I couldn't!"

I take a deep breath. "What do you think would have happened? Do you really think you would've died on the plane?"

Silence.

"Do you think that was an appropriate thing to say?" I prod.

"Oh, appropriate, appropriate! You have your version of things, I have mine."

"I remember what happened. You choose to forget."

"Maybe that is true."

It is my turn to fall silent. I contemplate her philosophic tone. I wonder how much she will ever acknowledge.

"Listen, Mom, I'm not mad at you. Obviously everything turned out okay. I'm just asking you to admit that you made a choice. It's not that you *couldn't* visit. You chose not to. The difference is important to me."

"If it is important to you, that is fine," she says. "Now tell me. What is Zoe up to these days?"

# 35

As summer turns to fall, she complains of being tired. She takes no pleasure from her job, filled with its administrative hassles. Her daily life sounds joyless. "Mom, why don't you go back to research? Call your old boss!" I suggest.

"I am too old for that," she mutters. "I just need to hang in there a bit longer."

I don't like how she sounds.

A few months later, after Zoe's first birthday, my mom retires, having worked just long enough to qualify for her pension. As always, she makes several decisions at once. She quits her job, sells her New Jersey house, and moves to the same Connecticut town as my brother. "Just in case anything were to happen," she explains.

Her whole life has been about averting disaster. What about pleasure?

"So what are you going to do now, with all your free time?" I ask.

"I don't want to do anything. I just want to rest."

"That might be nice at first, but you'll get bored."

"I never get bored."

"Come visit this summer," I offer. "I'll handle everything. You'll get to see Zoe. You won't have to lift a finger. The summers in Seattle are so great."

I hear her reluctance on the line.

"Is it the money?" I ask, confused. "Because I could use air-line miles and—"

"It is not the money!" she thunders.

I am taken aback. My mom never raises her voice.

"I should go," I say quickly.

"*Mayudi*—"

"No, no, it's okay." I shouldn't put her on the spot. It is the lesson my father tried to instill: I have to be less needy, less demanding. I must learn to be stronger than the people around me.

# 36

Noah starts traveling more for work. His trips to Japan usually last a week or two and are almost always at the last minute.

I want to be the mom who makes it look easy, casually alluding to a traveling spouse as though it's no big deal. I feel something else entirely: panic.

The panic isn't rational. I mostly handle Zoe's care on my own as it is, with Noah working all day. My anxiety stems from an idea planted by the depression. What if we *are* all alone in the world? I worry the demonic voice articulated a fundamental truth. I can't count on anyone.

My back pain flares up. "Are you okay?" neighbors ask, watching me hobble past. "Oh, sure." I force a smile as I lean on Zoe's stroller. "I'm fine!"

I call my mom to ask how retired life is treating her. I tell her about how I've been up since five A.M. with Zoe, how we have to walk Lola in the rain, how getting the stroller up and down the front steps with my bad back is tricky, but how none of it stops me from making the baby food from scratch or venturing to the zoo. I will never openly ask for her help again, but if I lay the guilt on thick enough, maybe she'll offer.

She does nothing of the kind. Instead she says, "Why don't you buy baby food like a normal person? Let Lola out into the yard. And hire a nanny!"

She doesn't understand. Taking care of Zoe doesn't bother me. What gets me is my isolation. How can the magic door between us have closed?

I can't say any of that, though—not when she had it so much harder. I want to be self-sufficient, but I don't know how to bear the loneliness. I'm not sure how to say that, either.

Everything I don't say comes out in my body. My back pain turns so acute that I develop a limp, sciatica zapping me with each step. I have to stand like a sumo wrestler to lift Zoe out of her crib. Every month, a new symptom flares. Hip bursitis, herniated lumbar discs, a torn rotator cuff, tendonitis, thoracic outlet syndrome: My medical file fattens. When a doctor suggests chronic stress as a culprit, I laugh mirthlessly. "I'm a mom," I say. He looks baffled.

My mom points out that things could be worse. "I had to use cloth diapers. Can you imagine, washing them? You have it so much easier!"

I feel rebuked. She is right. If she could do it, why can't I?

# 37

❧

There is a certain dark point at which self-sufficiency becomes a dare. Why ask for help when you can pretend not to need it? I start acting like the breezy mom. "Noah's gone for another two weeks," I say nonchalantly.

It turns out I get more sympathy when I pretend I'm not looking for it. "Two weeks!" friends exclaim. The more I airily insist I am fine, the more concern I get.

If I call my mom with charming stories of Zoe, she praises me. *Mayudi, Shanudi, Ranudi!* We are back in our zone of approval and affection. If I call her because I feel overwhelmed, she grows uncomfortable and hastily gets off the phone.

I begin to feed on this cycle, faking my feelings to get the reaction I crave. I take on tasks no sane person would attempt. I wash the exterior windows of the house, steam the curtains, and throw themed parties for the neighborhood kids, making all the food and decorations by hand.

"You don't have to do this, you know," says Noah, looking pained.

"I want to," I insist.

"What about your novel? Isn't the next step finding an agent? You should look into agents!"

Writing is one thing. Getting published is another. Researching the process, I was so daunted by what I learned that I decided to forget about my dream. Agents, editors. Who was I kidding?

Publishing feels out of reach not only because it is cutthroat, but for personal reasons as well. First-generation authors like me typically write about assimilation or the third world. My novel is about upper-crust privilege. When do Indian Americans ever write about WASPs? I am supposed to be on the outside looking in, not the inside looking out. Finding a publisher, already daunting, will be an uphill battle.

I focus instead on presiding over my perfect castle. I don't know if I can ever get an agent to represent me, but I can get my home to represent me pretty nicely.

I photograph my domestic efforts and post the results to social media. To the outside world, my life is a bright composite of artfully arranged food and festive parties, each post sweeping up heaps of "likes," which I study while applying an ice pack to my latest injury.

Being the perfect housewife fulfills something in me. I tell myself it is all for Zoe. I am giving her the sort of lovely, ordered home I never knew, an environment where she will feel nurtured. I tell myself that she prefers homemade baby food, that Lola's walks need to be at least thirty minutes long, that I have no choice in these matters. I back myself up against a wall no one else can see, just as my mom once did.

Perhaps my initial assumptions about motherhood were correct after all, and convenience and pleasure should be batted away. Self-sacrifice certainly feels like the right choice. The rewards are concrete: compliments, praise, "likes."

"Think of all the money we're saving!" I gloat to Noah.

"You don't seem happy," he says flatly.

What is happiness, exactly? I imagine the woman in the river felt some sliver of relief as the water rose above her. Sometimes it is strangely pleasant to drown oneself, to give into the current and watch the world recede.

# 38

My mom doesn't spend her retirement knitting or gardening. She doesn't visit my nieces or attend their birthday parties. She doesn't get together with relatives. As far as I can tell, she sits around all day watching television.

I pick up the phone and set it back down without dialing. The phone has become a phantom limb, a reminder of what was once there. Each time I reach for it, I feel bitter. *Oh,* I think. *Right.*

She and I no longer talk very much. When we do, I find myself acting superficially. I hear her relief. She doesn't want my reality. She wants the story that I am thriving.

If I ask her questions, I have to perform what I think of as the Hope Blockade, a conversational move for self-protection. The Hope Blockade involves not inquiring about her plans or alluding to the future because doing so is too painful. If I mention the holidays, for example, I have to face the fact that she doesn't want to visit. If I ask about her weekend plans, I have to acknowledge her apathy toward her kids and grandkids.

She sounds perfectly content. My brother and I trade notes about it.

"I mean, if she wants to spend her time watching TV, that's her choice."

"Right."

"Who's to say she's supposed to bake cookies with her grand-kids? That's a stereotype. As long as she's happy, good for her."

"Totally."

Sometimes he's the one talking himself out of his disappointment. Other times it's me. Either way, we chorus our agreement to hide our unease.

# 39

Over the next year, I start sending queries to literary agents. I don't tell a soul that I'm doing it. I'm too embarrassed. Then, just before Zoe's second birthday, I receive an offer of representation from an agent in New York.

Certain moments in life cause us to look up and reassess. The day I sign with my agent is one of them. It yanks me from my neatly stacked baby food purees and sparkling windows.

I see that I have been living in an illusion. I've created a fairy tale where home is picture-perfect, motherhood all-consuming, and martyrdom synonymous with bliss.

Signing that contract is terrifying. Going after my dream openly means there will be nowhere to hide. I think about how I once vowed never to hide behind Zoe. I ended up doing it anyway. It was so easy. I was rewarded for it.

Chasing a dream is harder. A long and lonely wait ensues after my agent sends my novel to publishers. There is nothing to joyously post about when the rejections begin to trickle in. After every major publisher turns my book down, I crumble.

I don't know what to do with my life. I interview for a couple of jobs I don't want. I listen glumly to friends' career advice. I do know what I want, of course. I want my dream. It just doesn't want me back.

I can't bring myself to call my mom for solace. Eventually,

after weeks of moping, I return to working on my novel. Giving it more of my time is hard to justify. I work on it because it's the only thing that makes me feel better.

It is a difficult time—gray Seattle skies, Noah traveling more and more, my mom and I talking less and less. I end up rewriting the book from scratch. It takes an additional year of work, the time carved out on weekends and weeknights.

My agent sends the revision to publishers. As I wait to hear back, checking email obsessively, refreshing the browser every few minutes, I wonder how much rejection a person can take. I sit up one night staring at the moon, worrying I've lost my grip on reality.

And then, just before Zoe's third birthday, in the middle of a ho-hum week, a chilly, bleak day when I've stop checking email because doing so is too painful, my agent calls to say there is interest. "Interest?" I repeat, not daring to breathe. "From multiple publishers," she reports happily. I have to lie down on the floor to take it in.

January 11, 2013. That is the day I sell my novel to a major publisher. That is the day my dream becomes real.

# 40

֍

"Mom, when you first came to this country . . . when you redid your residency . . . how did that work?"

"Hmm?"

"You had a six-month-old infant. Did you use daycare?"

"No, daycare did not exist back then."

I roll my eyes. Of course daycare *existed,* but this is what she does. She puts up walls. "So what did you do?"

"Why are you asking?"

"My editor wants me to revise my novel. My first big deadline is coming up. Noah's going to be away for the next two and a half months for a trial. I looked into daycares, but they have wait lists. Nannies cost too much. I don't know what to do."

"Well, at least your hours are flexible. You don't have to be on call."

"I know, I know." I feel a familiar wave of guilt. "It's just . . . I keep wondering how people do this. How *you* did it."

"I don't know," she says, as always. "I just did."

# 41

*If my mom could do it, so can I.*

This becomes my mantra during the next two and a half months.

By now, Zoe is old enough for preschool, but the hours are short: nine A.M. to one P.M. It isn't enough time. I hire a sitter for a few hours. It's still not enough.

I finally hit on a solution: I stay up all night. Staying up, I find, is perfect. The house is quiet, Zoe is asleep, and there are no interruptions, no dishwasher to unload or dog to walk. I don't even need coffee. My novel is going to be published! The adrenaline alone keeps me going.

I work until I hear Zoe stir. Then I get her ready, drive her to preschool, and sleep from nine-thirty to twelve-thirty. I care for Zoe the rest of the day, taking her to parks and the library, making her dinner, giving her a bath, putting her to bed. I then watch bad television in a vegetative state for an hour or two in the belief that this, like a medically induced coma, will restore me. At ten o'clock, I drag my laptop out and stay up all over again.

There are times I think I might fall over from exhaustion, times I show up for preschool pickup looking deranged, times I try to put in a contact lens only to find one already in my eye.

Through all of it, I think of my mom, doing her residency while washing cloth diapers in a foreign country. Surely she worked even harder. Surely she slept even less. I repeat my mantra: *If my mom could do it, so can I.*

And so I do.

# 42

"What did you end up doing when Noah was gone?" my mom asks after I turn in my edits. "Did you hire a nanny? Or find a daycare?"

"Nope," I say proudly. I share my ingenious nocturnal routine.

*"What?"* My mom is appalled. "You can't do that!"

"Well," I say with a little laugh, "what choice did I have? Besides, it worked out. You were the one who inspired me, actually."

"But this is unsafe! You have not been sleeping!"

"Come on, Mom, you must have pulled all-nighters when you were a resident."

"That was out of necessity!"

"And this isn't? This is for my career."

That gives her pause.

"I thought you'd be proud," I continue blankly. "I'm doing what you did."

"Oh!" Her voice is anguished. "I never thought . . . I never imagined . . . I should be *ashamed.*"

"Mom, why would you say that?"

"I should have come," she mumbles. "I should have been there."

I have no idea what she's talking about. When I was suicidal, she was absent. Now that I've succeeded in handling everything on my own, she feels remorse. This must be misplaced guilt.

"Listen, Mom, I'm fine. Seriously! I mean, granted, it wasn't easy, but I made it work. What you said all along was right. I have no idea how I did it. I just did."

I expect her to laugh. She doesn't.

"This is nothing like before," I assure her. "When I was depressed or whatever. I'm fine now. I'm good!"

She sounds shaken when we get off the phone.

Her guilt makes no sense to me.

# 43

After Noah has spent ten weeks on the road, he has a few days home before leaving for yet another business trip. We try to reconnect by going out to dinner.

I tell him a story about how my friend, Shannon, brought over a bottle of champagne to celebrate my book deal. "Wait," he says, "who's Shannon again?" He tells me about a witness he deposed in Texas. "You went to *Texas*?" I ask. "When was this?" We look at each other, troubled by our disconnect.

"I want to change jobs," he finally says. "The travel . . . it's too much. I'm missing all of Zoe's milestones. I hate not being here. I looked at listings on the East Coast. Nothing's the right fit."

We both miss New York. Seattle has never felt like home.

"I don't want you to apply for jobs that don't excite you," I say. "So what do we do?"

I don't know how to answer, so I follow the basic recipe for reassurance: a lie followed by a platitude followed by a lie. "Maybe your travel will ease up. We'll figure it out. Maybe we'll start to like Seattle."

He smiles. It's our running joke. Seattle is a place that grows on you. Four years in, we're still waiting for that to happen.

# 44

"What are you doing for the holidays?"

"Mom, we're coming to visit you. Remember?"

"Oh! How wonderful!"

It is October, Zoe now a vivacious pre-kindergartner who loves science and math and resists my efforts to encourage artsier pursuits. "I pwe-fuh nonfiction," she tells me at the library in her little Elmer Fudd voice. She is a constant, joyous surprise.

My mom, however, predictably irritates me. While I once looked to her for solace in the early days of caring for my daughter, it is now Zoe who brings me comfort after each difficult conversation with my mom.

I remind my mom of the dates of our visit. I have her write them down. She doesn't pay close enough attention when we speak. I often hear the TV blaring in the background.

I ask what she had for dinner, my new go-to question devised by the Hope Blockade. If I ask what she's been up to, she mumbles, "Nothing," in a dull voice and I grow annoyed. At least the subject of food is neutral.

She tells me about the takeout she picked up. She never used to get takeout, even when she was juggling two kids and a demanding career. I listen as she describes a dish of eggplant and black beans from the Chinese place where they know her by name.

"So tell me," she says. "What are you doing for the holidays?"

I freeze.

"Hello?" she says.

"M-m-mom," I stammer. "*Mom*. We're coming to visit you."

"Oh! How wonderful! When?"

Shakily, I repeat the dates. I wait for her to say, "Oh, that's right, we just went through this." I wait for her to say, "Silly me! I was distracted—I have the TV on, you know." She says none of those things.

I call my brother. "Have you noticed any issues with Mom recently? With her memory?"

"Yeah, actually. I've been meaning to mention it."

While he shares a similar episode and tries to downplay it ("I mean, it's probably nothing, right?"), I see what my mom has been trying to tell me. She said it that one afternoon when I stared at the neighbor's cedar. She's been saying it ever since.

She needs help.

This whole time, I thought I was the one who was drowning. It never occurred to me that she was.

She wanted a false story from me. Without realizing it, I wanted one from her. We've been hiding from each other. We each wanted to believe the other was fine.

That same week, Noah tells me about a job listing in New York. The job, he says, sounds perfect.

I have never been one to read into events, to talk about "the universe" or "signs," to see myself as the epicenter of anything, but the timing of that job listing feels oddly fated.

He flies to New York for interviews. Even as he talks about the other talented candidates, the fact that I shouldn't get my hopes up, I know he'll get the offer.

This is my story's arc, to return to my mother. I can't say what our relationship will look like, but I have the unshakable feeling that this is the right thing to do.

We put our house on the market.

It sells in three days.

Just like that, we're heading home.

II

# 1

A perk of being back east is that Zoe gets to see her beloved cousins, as we often visit my brother on weekends. We're renting a furnished apartment in White Plains, just outside of New York City, and though the rental is an anonymous shell, though the heating is unreliable and often not up to the task of battling winter's frigid temperatures, our situation feels vastly improved. Zoe now attends a preschool with other minority children. I get to see my family whenever I want. Something in me relaxes. The piles of slush on the sidewalk, the honking of cars in traffic, the crowded subway when I venture into the city to meet my editor: They make me smile, for they are mine, and I have missed them. Visiting my brother's house only affirms my contentment, until I call my mom.

"Why don't you join us?"

"Eh. I'm tired."

"Do you want one of us to get you?"

"No," she says, hanging up.

My brother and I don't know how to react: what to make of her memory lapses (which are infrequent), if we should be worried (a question we're not sure how to answer), or whether we should respect her desire to be left alone.

Sometimes we show up to get her and, despite her protests, she has a great time. Other times she joins us only to fall asleep on the couch. Occasionally, she grows resentful and claims we're trying to control her. This happens so rarely that it's easy to chalk up to a bad mood. Besides which, she's right. We *are* trying to control her.

We've started saying things like, "C'mon, Mom, it'll be good for you," and, "When's the last time you left the house?" It feels patronizing.

We begin to think twice about inviting her. We tell ourselves not to take her ambivalence personally, but shouldn't she want to spend time with us? Even when she comes along, she does so without enthusiasm. It stings.

Who is she without us? She was always focused on her kids. Now we're the ones focused on her. As we try to gauge her needs, the uncertainty of our roles is the hardest part. We no longer have our old scripts.

She has mood swings. I think of them as Mom Roulette. The ball typically settles somewhere safe (Tired Mom, Vaguely Pleasant Mom), but occasionally it lands on Paranoid Mom or Accusatory Mom. These cameos, however rare, are unnerving.

Is this early Alzheimer's? My brother and I discuss it. Noah and I discuss it. We are out of our depth, like children discussing grown-up matters, alternately thrilled and terrified to be talking about what we do not understand.

Alzheimer's brings to my mind a dotty old woman wandering the streets in a pink bathrobe, needing to be led by the elbow back home. None of that applies to my mother. She cleans, cooks, drives, handles her finances, and in most ways is as sharp and put-together as ever. Even using the word *Alzheimer's* feels fraudulent. Surely some degree of memory loss and grumpiness comes with age.

"I mean, even if it *is* Alzheimer's," my brother argues, "what's the next step? A nursing home? An aide? She's not ready for any of that."

I agree. "We'd know if anything bad were to happen. Leaving the stove on or getting lost. There'd be warning signs."

As a precaution, we put her bills on autopay. "Just in case," my brother explains to her. "This way there's no risk of forgetting to write the checks."

*Just in case.* Her whole life was oriented around those three words. How strange to be anticipating the future on her behalf.

# 2

We are happy to be back in New York, but life also feels oddly suspended. Our apartment is temporary. My novel comes out in six months. I don't know what to make of my mom's symptoms, if they should even be called that. I'm waiting to see where everything will land, myself included.

When friends ask where we plan to live, I admit that I'm not sure. When they ask about my mom, I confess that I don't know what to think—that while nothing terrible has happened, she isn't herself. I once would have yearned to sound in control. I find myself less concerned with appearances.

The obvious next step would be to take my mom to a doctor, but my brother and I keep putting it off. We don't know how to take charge. On medical matters, she insists she knows best.

My mom wasn't your run-of-the-mill psychiatrist. With triple board certifications in psychiatry, geriatrics, and pharmacology, she is an expert on the aging brain. Suggesting she see a doctor would be like telling a master carpenter to go to IKEA.

We finally convince her to see someone by pointing out that she's lost weight, enough that she's been folding her pants over at the waist.

"I suppose I should have my thyroid function tested," she concedes.

My brother takes her to an internist, who begins the appointment by asking her a few casual questions.

My mom snorts. "Are you trying to assess my cognitive function? I will save you the trouble. I have early onset dementia."

My brother is stunned. "Mom, if you knew this, why didn't you say anything?"

"What is there to say? Dementia is dementia. Your *agi* had it in India. There was nothing we could do for her. Little has changed since then."

The internist raises the subject of medication. My mom cuts her off, rattling off each drug's limitations and side effects. "Medication is of little value. There is no treatment for dementia. I know this better than anyone."

"What about your weight loss?" my brother interjects. "I'm worried you're forgetting to eat."

"I am not forgetting. I am lazy! It is hard to cook for just one person. I will make more of an effort."

"We'll check your weight again in six months," the doctor finally cedes. "But if it hasn't gone up—"

"It will! You will see! I will be plump!" My mom laughs and picks up her purse, leading the way out.

# 3

For Mother's Day, Noah, Zoe, and I drive up to Connecticut to take my mom out to dinner. She doesn't look thrilled to see us. "I don't want to go out," she grouses. "Let's not cause a scene in front of Zoe," I coax. Grumbling, she puts on her shoes.

The restaurant has the charming feel of a bed-and-breakfast: wide-planked floors, rolled tin ceilings, candles on each table. "Ooh," murmurs Zoe appreciatively. My mom does not reply. Roulette that night has yielded Sullen Mom, who glares at the waiter reading the specials.

I order a martini. Normally I don't drink in front of my mom, but tonight I need one. I can't bear to see her so withdrawn.

"Grandma," announces Zoe, "I have *many* cool things to tell you."

If my mother's mood is a gamble, my daughter's mood is a sure thing. She is the most enthusiastic child I have ever encountered, lit with energy, brimming over with life, and enthralled by her grandmother's favorite subject: science.

"Did you know, Grandma, that an electric eel can make enough electricity to power ten lightbulbs?"

Grandma doesn't answer.

"Wow," I say quickly, "I didn't know that! That's amazing!"

How can my mom ignore her own grandchild? Why is having a meal with her such a chore? She doesn't ask me about my

upcoming book tour, doesn't ask Noah about his job. I am reminded of meals with my dad.

Dinner with my mom isn't supposed to feel this way. It should
be a wonderful evening. The food is delicious. Zoe is so sweet.
She keeps raising her little glass of juice to toast us. It's a bit like
having dinner with the sun and the clouds at the same table, one
dazzling and radiant, the other dark and sulky.

I order a second martini.

Noah glances at me with concern. I never have two martinis.

Meanwhile, my mom eats. She polishes off our appetizers, all
of her entrée, and the shared desserts. This is why we've taken
her out. We want her to have a square meal. Yet every time her
trembling fork comes forward, quavering in the air because of a
hand tremor she has developed, I feel annoyed. She has more
enthusiasm for the tiramisu than for Zoe.

She doesn't comment on the food. She doesn't thank us for
dinner. She hardly speaks.

After we drop her off at her house, I exhale my relief. From
the passenger seat, I lower the window and breathe the cool
night air. I am glad to be free of her, but filled with guilt for feeling that way.

Through the side mirror, my eyes travel to Zoe. I don't want
her to see me blue. "I think we should have a dance party," I an-
nounce. I put on some music, Beyoncé and Prince. We sing the
words, dancing in our seats, and soon I am laughing, not for my
daughter's sake, but for mine.

# 4

After seven months in our rental apartment, we buy a house. A 1920s colonial in need of updates and a new roof, it is none of the things we said we wanted, but it is in a town we love.

A sleepy village tucked away on the Hudson, the town has the quaint feel and slow rhythms of another era. The main street is actually called Main Street. The river at its base is a mesmerizing swath of blue gray.

I have never lived in such a place. The residents all know one another. I learn to stop tapping my foot in line at the coffee shop because the person in front of me inevitably turns out to be a neighbor.

"I want to see this place!" my mom announces. "When can I come?"

"Oh," I say, surprised. She recently stopped driving. Nothing happened, no incident where she got lost or forgot where she parked. She simply decided it was time. She made the decision in her typically oblique way, delivering the outcome, not what led to it, no matter that the decision has serious ramifications. Now that she doesn't drive, it falls to my brother to bring her food.

"I can pick you up one of these days," I offer. It's a busy time. I'm traveling for author events, Zoe has her preschool graduation, and there's the matter of the dozens of cardboard boxes our moving company delivered that I desperately need to unpack.

"Pick me up? That will be so inconvenient for you! There must be a train. Do you know? Does one exist?"

"Well, yeah, but I thought it might be too much. . . ."

"What is there to worry about?" Her voice is playful and cavalier. "We can pin a note to my shirt so the conductor knows to help me."

I laugh despite myself. It is unlike her to acknowledge her need for help. Mom Roulette today has yielded Cheerful Mom. I welcome the change.

"Look into it for me," she continues. "I want to see your house!"

As always, I do as she instructs. I find a foolproof route. My brother and I discuss the arrangements as though we are in charge of a small child.

She sounds apprehensive as the day approaches. "Do I need to remember the name of the station? Do I need to transfer?"

"You don't," I assure her. My brother will put her on the right train. I'll be waiting on the other end. "All you have to do is stay on until the last stop."

The night before her arrival, I prepare a vegetable curry with sweet potatoes and coconut milk, fragrant and warming. Zoe makes a "welcome" sign and hangs it from the mantel.

At dawn, I wake to the buzzing of my phone. "I've been up all night," she says, agitated. "A train! At my age! I could get lost. There might be muggers! You cannot expect such things of me. I don't know why you thought of it."

Once, I would have protested. I would have said it was all her idea, that she won't get lost, that there is nothing to worry about. Now I know better.

"It's okay, Mom. I understand."

She starts to argue before my words register. "You—you do?"

"You shouldn't do anything that stresses you out."

She is quiet a long moment. "Thank you for understanding, *Mayudi*. I thought you would be disappointed."

I am, though. Of course I am.

I take my frustration out on a stack of cardboard boxes. I unpack them noisily, hacking at the tape. "I can't wait till this place feels more like home," I mutter.

"It does feel like home, Mommy," says Zoe.

Does it? I haven't yet located her stuffed animals, hidden in one of the many boxes labeled MISC. The rooms feel bare, everything a mess.

What bothers me has nothing to do with unpacking, of course. I hadn't realized how much I was looking forward to the visit until my mom canceled. I should be past the point of expecting anything from her. I should be past the point of hope. Yet here I am, acting childish around my child, who ate a plateful of rice and curry for dinner and deemed it delicious. I mixed yogurt and sugar into her portion, but still, I wonder if she is trying to make me feel better—if, pre-kindergarten, she has already assumed this responsibility.

"What makes it feel that way?" I ask, curious. "What does home mean to you?"

Zoe considers the question for a long moment. Then she says, "Home is where you go when everything is closed. Like when Ben and Jerry's is closed and the park is closed and the library is closed, you go home. Home is the place that's always open."

It's a lovely definition, more wonderful than anything I could have conjured. It dawns on me that when my mom's behavior first changed, when we stopped speaking as much by phone, I turned to housework. I told myself my efforts were for Zoe, but that isn't quite right. I was trying to make up for a hole in my life.

My mom was the one who made me feel at home in the world. She was the person always available to me when the rest of the world felt closed off. After she refused to visit me in Seattle, I lost my magic door. I've been trying to find a sense of belonging ever since.

When my mom finally does see the house, it is because I drive to Connecticut to get her. "It's so nice here," she comments, "but next time I should take the train. There must be a train. Do you know? Does one exist? Look into it for me."

# 5

"Y ou are famous!"

"Mom, I'm not famous."

"You have a bestseller!"

My book isn't selling very well, but I don't interrupt as she goes on rapturously about my novel. My big fear leading up to the release was that she wouldn't remember it, an idea that seemed too terrible to contemplate. If an achievement takes place and your mom isn't there to notice it, does it really happen?

My brother brought her to one of my author events. Far from forgetting it, she misremembers vividly. "I watched you onstage. There were hundreds of people!" On any given day, she is capable of wild fabrications. "Oprah loved your book!" "It is number one on Amazon!" No amount of correcting her can set the record straight. To her, I'm a celebrity. It should be touching, but it feels grotesque and sad, her memory full of distortions. "You are famous!" She beams. I grimace and change the subject.

# 6

A necessary part of life is casting it aside on occasion. Books, movies, food, sex: All offer not merely entertainment but existential exit. We call our ideal television watching experience "vegging out." We put ourselves in "food comas." Comedians cause us to "die" of laughter. The French refer to orgasm as *la petite mort*. I've often wondered about this flirtation with death. It's not that we want to be gone. We just want—briefly—for life to stop. It's what Robert Frost means when he describes climbing birches: the desire to "get away from earth awhile / And then come back to it and begin over." I crave that feeling more than ever as I witness my mother's decline.

Novels have always been my escape of choice. They offer the ultimate transportive high. A good dealer knows his product but also views it as such. "I need a new hobby," I tell people. I will always read incessantly, but it's no longer a release. It's my job. Friends suggest knitting, podcasts, gardening—all sorts of activities, none of which feels right. I want something more intense. I want oblivion.

I'm watching football one Sunday when a Play 60 ad comes on, encouraging kids to exercise. My eyes travel to Zoe, hunched over a book. Of course she is. Nurture and nature's one-two punch has resulted in this, my beautiful, bespectacled girl whose shoulders have already started to round at her tender single-digit age.

I glance back at the TV. Kids swarm a green field. When's the last time my daughter played for an hour, not at school or camp but freely? If someone handed me a survey, I'd check the box that says I value fitness, but what do I do to model it? My hobbies have always been sedentary: reading, writing, cooking.

I think back to when I was last fit: my wedding day. It's not just that I was skinny. I was in shape. I did push-ups. I sprinted hills. I felt great. At the time, it bothered me that it took getting engaged to get fit. I wondered why squeezing into a dress motivated me more than the worthy goal of self-care. How can I think that and not do anything about it?

I decide to join a gym—and not just any gym, but a nice one. I don't want fitness to be punishment. I swallow my guilt about the cost and look into hiring a trainer. "I want someone who's experienced," I say. "No twenty-year-olds."

The gym manager smiles. "I think I have just the person."

This is how I meet Louis, who has olive skin and a black moustache and looks to be in his forties. "What are you looking to accomplish?" he asks.

I call up the little talk I've rehearsed on the way over. "I want to be fit," I reply, "but not in a way that's about weight loss or size. I want, um, a positive relationship to fitness."

I don't know what I expect—incredulity? laughter?—but Louis nods. "Is there anything you've always wanted to do? A goal you'd like to accomplish?"

Right away, I know the answer, but I don't want to say it aloud. I shift my feet. He waits. "Well . . . I've always wanted to do a pull-up. I mean, I know they're really hard for women, and they might be out of the question for me—"

"We can get you doing pull-ups."

"Plural?" I laugh.

"Plural," he affirms. He points to the pull-up bar at the center of the gym floor. "We'll have you hopping up there and doing sets of them. Pull-up after pull-up."

I look at him dubiously. He sounds sincere. He seems like the type of person who doesn't make promises lightly.

"Why not?" he continues, as though reading my thoughts. "Don't spend your time doubting. Spend your time doing." It becomes one of many aphorisms I file away: Lou-isms, as I soon come to think of them.

We head to the pull-up assist. The higher the setting, the more assistance you get. The very fit man who hops off the machine as we approach has it at a five. To my horror, Louis moves the peg down to a twelve. I scowl as I step onto the platform.

"Ah. So we're motivated by numbers. Do you know how old I am?"

I shrug. "Forty?"

He smiles. "I'm sixty."

*What?* You could knock me over with a feather in that moment. The man is sculpted as a statue. It makes no sense that he is only a few years younger than my mom.

"I'm a grandpa," he continues wryly. "Sixty. It's a number. We don't let numbers get us down."

Well. What is my twelve to his sixty? I climb up and manage five reps. When I stop, I expect him to yell at me, but he says, "Good! I saw you fighting for that last one. That's excellent."

Louis isn't one for small talk, which I appreciate. He focuses on my form, though I get the feeling that as he gently corrects my technique ("knees track over the toes when you squat"), he's doing something more. He's reading me.

"You want to get things right on the first try," he observes. "You need to remember that fitness is a process."

He points to the scariest apparatus on the floor, a white cage with a horizontal metal bar. "That's a squat rack. The bar on its own is forty-five pounds. Soon we'll have you doing squats with real weight."

"How much do you squat?" I ask, curious.

"Six hundred and forty pounds."

I choke on my water.

"Time," he says. "Strength is a result of effort and time."

"The thing is, with my back problems—"

I've already told him my medical history: the herniated discs and sciatica.

"You know the reason for your back pain?"

"Um, my back is weak?"

He shakes his head. "Your lower back is strong. It's been over-compensating." He regards me. "We shouldn't ask so much of any one part. Too much strength can be its own weakness, you know."

I blink. Are we discussing the body? Or is this another Lou-ism? I open my mouth to speak, but Louis has already moved on to the next exercise.

# 7

Several months after my mother's appointment with the internist, things seem to have stabilized. She promises she is eating heartily. Her symptoms haven't worsened, as far as my brother and I can discern.

Part of me is secretly relieved to know about her condition. I finally understand why she couldn't visit me in Seattle. Perhaps I can't count on her the way I used to, but the possibility still exists of connecting as mother and daughter.

On Alzheimer's websites, I learn that patients enjoy being asked about the past. To my surprise, I find this to be true of my mom. She was always so guarded, but dementia can involve a loosening of inhibitions, the cognitive equivalent of a glass of wine.

"I keep thinking about when you first came to this country," I remark one day on the phone with her. "It must have been so hard."

"Oh yes," she recalls dreamily. "Between shifts at the hospital, I would nap in the break room. You learn to sleep standing up as a resident! If I had time, I would run home and gulp down the lunch my mother had made. She scolded me for eating too fast, but I did not have time to sit down."

"Your mother?" I repeat. "Wait, you must mean during medical school."

"No, this was in my residency."

"But you . . . you did your residency here in the States."

"Well, you know, my parents came for a bit. Anyway—"

"Hang on." I'm confused. How could *Agi* have prepared her lunch here in America? "What do you mean, your parents came for a bit?" I ask suspiciously.

"When my program began, my parents came to help me."

"For how long?"

"A year."

"*A year?* Mom, you never said anything about this."

"Well, how else was I supposed to manage? Your brother was a baby."

"Yeah, I'm clear on that part. You just . . . you never said anything about . . ." I shake my head in frustration. "Was that the plan all along, that they'd join you?"

"No." She sighs. "You have to understand, when I arrived in this country, it was very difficult. I did not understand one word of what people were saying. I had never cooked or even made my own tea, I was so used to servants—"

"Mom, you've told me all this."

"One afternoon, I called my parents in tears. It was the middle of the night in Bombay. I said I could not manage on my own, that it was too much. They offered to get on a plane and come."

A desperate phone call. Feeling overwhelmed and alone. Wanting—needing—support. I am speechless.

"They left everything behind," she continues, oblivious to my stunned silence. "Your father and I were living in a small apartment in Queens at the time. It was not meant for so many people. Still, my parents stayed with us. For a whole year they took care of your brother. They took care of everything."

Some part of me wants to yell that she got to have what I

didn't. Another part of me wants to get the story while the getting is good. I clear my throat. "What happened next? I mean, your residency lasted longer than a year."

"They took your brother back to India with them."

"For—for how long?"

She answers in a small voice, "Until he was five."

"*What?* Mom, that can't be true."

"What do you mean? Of course it is true."

"Manish didn't live in India."

"He absolutely did."

I run my hand through my hair. "So let me get this straight. You came here when Manish was six months old. Your parents arrived to help soon after. They stayed here for a year. And then they took him back to India *until he was five*?"

"Correct."

"So you were on your own for, what, a couple of months?"

A meek noise of assent.

"Why didn't you tell me? The whole time I was in Seattle, you knew I was struggling."

"I didn't think it mattered. What good would it do?"

"You didn't think it *mattered*?" My voice is so high it feels like it's coming out of the crown of my head. "I asked you! I specifically *asked* you how you did it! And you said, 'I don't know. I just did.' Those were your exact words! You never said, 'I had help, that's how.' Or, 'Because I didn't actually raise him—' "

"I called!" she interrupts hotly. "At least once a month, I called! Do you know how expensive international phone calls were back then?"

I laugh. I can't help it. I don't even try to keep the derision out of my voice. "That's how you defend your parenting? With a once-a-month phone call?"

"I had no choice! You have to understand!"

"Of course you had choices! You could have put your career on hold. You could have delayed your residency."

"No, no, those were not options at the time."

I snort. "Mom, just because you didn't want to consider them, it doesn't mean they didn't exist." I pace the room like an attorney during a cross-examination. "You always described that as the hardest time of your life. . . ."

"Yes."

"When you called your parents, they came to help. But when I called you, you refused. Not only did you *not* help me, you created a fiction that you'd done everything yourself. All those times I called you when I was struggling, all those times I felt guilty for not being able to manage on my own—"

"Enough. I did the best I could. I'm sorry that isn't enough for you."

"*Please.*" I want nothing to do with her martyrdom. For once, I want her to take ownership of her actions. "You hid this from me."

"I did no such thing. It never occurred to me to tell you."

"Is that really how you look at this? Or is that just the version that makes you feel better?"

"The only reason I became a doctor was for my children. Everything I do is for my children!"

"Oh God, Mom. You know, I might be the writer," I say, for I can never resist the parting shot, the final word, "but you're the one with the gift for stories."

# 8

Now that I have this knowledge, what am I supposed to do with it?

Am I supposed to feel good about having done what she couldn't?

I don't.

I regret doubting my abilities as a mother. I feel naïve for having been duped so easily. Mainly, though, I am angry.

I remember when I needed Caren and the shrink and Noah to be livid on my behalf, their indignation fanning the flames of my newfound anger. This time, I can see my mother's deception for myself. My fury now is all my own.

My mom and I had stood in the same river. She didn't tell me about the rescue boat that arrived to save her. She left it out even when I asked her how she swam. Exhausted, I blamed myself for not being stronger.

This is the legacy of myths. They set an impossible standard. They are alluring for precisely the same reason they are dangerous: They refuse to disclose details. Yet those details, so pesky to myths, are where life occurs. The details tell the true story. The myth is the story as it wishes it could be.

# 9

The next time I talk to my brother, I ask him about it. "I have sort of a weird question for you," I say tentatively. "Do you, um, know that you lived in India until you were five?"

He laughs. "Of course I know. Why do you ask?"

I explain about Mom's confession. "The whole thing was such a shock to me, I thought it might be news to you. You always say you don't remember your childhood."

"It's not that I don't remember it at all, just that it's fuzzy. But, yeah, that's why I was close with *Ajoba* and *Agi*."

"So all those summers you went to visit them . . ." I let the sentence trail off. "I thought Mom and Dad liked you more. I thought that's why you got to fly to India by yourself."

"That never occurred to me. I thought of you as the lucky one for being born here."

He's right, of course. I *was* the lucky one. I never had to deal with a citizenship test or the arduous process of becoming naturalized. I was simply American.

"When you came to the States, it must have been so hard," I reflect. "That was, what, right before kindergarten?"

"Yeah, but you know how kids are. You roll with stuff. I remember standing in the airport and having Mom and Dad pointed out to me. I had this funny feeling, like, 'Oh, those are my parents. I've heard about them.'"

I shake my head. I can't imagine it. "Did you even speak English?"

"I'm not sure. I don't remember taking special classes or anything."

My brother sounds completely American when he speaks. No one would ever guess he grew up in India. The thought makes me laugh. Not even I knew.

"Do you hold it against Mom?" I ask after a beat. "That she sent you away like that?"

"Not at all. It must have been incredibly hard for her. Besides, I have no complaints. I loved it over there."

I can't tell if he's philosophically making the best of his situation or if he genuinely feels this way.

I grew up with the understanding that the past was off-limits. It seems my brother did, too. My whole family avoided the subject. I have no idea how this unspoken pact was formed. Whenever I visit Noah's family, I am astonished by their nostalgia, the teasing and reminiscing. My family could never do this. Even the occasional fond memory is tied up in our dysfunction.

Learning about my brother's childhood ignites a spark, like the striking of a match. I'm not only learning about my mom. I'm realizing how long I've been in the dark.

# 10

Until now, I had believed my mom represented the apex of maternal wisdom. I viewed her choices as a nearly mystical combination of unconditional love and psychiatric expertise. She was a brilliant mother who knew what she was doing. She had to be.

I wanted so badly for someone to be in charge of me. With one recognizably bad parent in my dad, I needed my mom to make up for him.

So what if she didn't leave him? Surely she knew things I didn't. So what if she didn't seek out help for me after my suicide attempt? Maybe she didn't want it on my record. I invented reasons to defend her. I generated stories in my head to explain why her actions were in my best interests.

I see now what the shrink tried to show me during our sessions. I gave my mom credit even when I had to twist logic to do so. I was so determined to have a mythic mom that I invented one.

Understanding this is like having blinders ripped off. I see what I didn't want to previously acknowledge.

All along, it was me. I was the one tending to myself. I was the one who rescued myself from my dad. I gave myself what I needed.

Her nonreaction on the piano bench, the way she went along

with my plan to go to boarding school, the way she refused to budge when I begged her to come to Seattle—I made a choice to view her as encouraging me to stand on my own two feet.

What if I came home one day to find Zoe terrorized? I would never stand idly by. I would never take her out for ice cream instead of talking with her. I would never let her languish in a college dorm room if she were depressed. I would do everything in my power to help her. I would do what wasn't done for me.

I had thought of my mom's refusal to visit me in Seattle as an aberration, a strange blip in an otherwise uninterrupted history of maternal love. I yearned to believe that she had always been there for me, my safety net, but I had been wrong. Her refusal to see me when I was in the depths of postpartum depression was just another in a life's worth of choices made in favor of what was best, most convenient, for her.

Upon learning of her dementia, some part of me had been relieved. It was the part of me that didn't want to confront reality.

Alzheimer's wasn't the reason she didn't visit me. It just removed her ability to cover for herself. In the past, she would have sold her choice more convincingly. She would have told a better story.

"Everything I do is for my children." She said the words because she wanted to believe them. I wanted to believe them, too.

# 11

As I take in what I've learned, I struggle to fathom her decision to send my brother to India for all those years. How do I reconcile her choices with how I wish to see her?

When I was growing up, my family would often get together with relatives. One family in particular stands out. The wife, an accomplished physicist, gave up her career when they immigrated to the States. The husband was a surgeon. Someone needed to look after the kids. "Where's her backbone?" I once asked my mom. "She must be so bored, home all day, cooking and cleaning." My mom shushed me and told me not to say such things. I had no idea that one day I'd share the same fate, a PhD chopping carrots and changing diapers.

*We must not judge the woman in the river.*

This, too, was what she said. She said it with a sigh, maybe because she knew about being judged, about the futility of asking not to be. I'd liked the idea of the woman in the river choosing herself, yet here I am, judging my mom for having done exactly that.

It seems the woman in the river can't choose correctly. Choosing herself, she faces judgment. Sacrificing herself, she faces it, too. That is the real lesson of the story: A woman faces judgment no matter what she chooses. No wonder my mom hid the truth from me.

*I never thought . . . I never imagined . . . I should be* ashamed. Her anguish upon learning of my all-nighters comes back to me. Her words made no sense at the time. Now they do.

She refused to consider that her silence about her past would have consequences. She was evasive on the subject of motherhood because she didn't want to admit to having sent my brother to India. She didn't want to dwell on a painful decision. *I just want to move forward,* I once told the shrink. My mom felt that way, too. We had tried moving forward by denying the past.

She was reluctant to give up the story, one we had both built. She *wanted* to be the woman who sacrificed herself for her children. She and I were united in this desire.

The legacy of her silence caught up with her when she learned of my all-nighters. She assumed I would get the help I needed, the same way she had. She never dreamed that by failing to mention the support she'd received, I would feel guilty for needing it. She didn't realize that in omitting her struggles, I would question the legitimacy of mine. She didn't see that a mother's story affects a daughter's choices.

Shame prevented her from speaking about that time. Shame leads to silence. This is its real triumph, not the guilt we carry, but that we move forward without saying a word.

# 12

It is a blessing and a curse that life continues when we most need it to stop. Whatever my feelings about my mother, her needs persist. At her next checkup, despite all of her confident assurances that she would be plump, her weight has dropped. She is down to a hundred pounds.

Even she can't argue with the numbers. Reluctantly, she agrees to take Aricept, an Alzheimer's medication thought to slow memory decline. My brother buys a special alarmed pill-box designed for Alzheimer's patients. The box is billed as foolproof.

He and I redouble our efforts. He brings her extra helpings of takeout, going out of his way to get food she likes: *chana masala* from the good Indian place in Branford, pasta from the Italian caterer in Madison. I cook meals and fill her fridge. I label everything in big letters so she won't get confused about what it is or when it's from.

I call her at mealtimes. "Did you eat lunch? There are homemade black bean burgers in your fridge." "Oh yes," she says. "They were delicious!" Sometimes she sounds groggy when she picks up. My brother reports she's often asleep when he drops by. "Daytime napping, I guess," he says.

We constantly wonder how worried we should be. The two of us are on eggshells. We don't want to offend her. We don't want to overreact. She assures us she is fine. We have no idea how to gauge parental competence. Books and blogs abound for how to parent my child. How do I parent my parent?

She calls my brother one day to express her sadness that he won't let her buy a piano. "What are you talking about, Mom? You've never mentioned anything about a piano." "Oh," she says. "I think I had a dream about it. Silly me! I was just confused."

She calls me one afternoon to say she's been robbed, her gold jewelry missing from her bureau. I help her track it down. It's in the bathtub. "You must think I am so dumb," she says sheepishly. "I hid it there when the handyman came, just to be safe. Then I forgot."

She calls relatives in the middle of the night, convinced of some emergency. She calls her bank and cancels her credit cards. My brother and I intervene, explaining, smoothing, fixing, righting her world into order.

These events occur months apart. We assure ourselves that their lack of frequency makes them less troubling.

"I've had the same thing happen, where you have a vivid dream and then think it's real," says my brother.

"I guess the bathtub makes sense as a hiding place," I hear myself remark. "It's actually kind of clever."

This is how we reassure each other, how we reassure ourselves, except that none of it is terribly reassuring.

Finally, we make an appointment at the Adler Geriatric Center in New Haven, which specializes in dementia. From our very first phone call, it is clear that this is different from a typical doctor's office. We don't have to explain that the appointment is for someone else, that the patient is unwilling, that she might even get combative. They already know.

# 13

We meet with our assigned caseworker, Kathy, while my mom has her vitals checked.

"So what brings you here?" Kathy asks. "Tell me about your mom."

My brother and I both begin speaking at once.

"Well, she's started doing this thing where—"

"Recently she's been a little confused about—"

We glance at each other and laugh uneasily. There is so much to say.

Talking with Kathy is like talking to a magician. She instantly divines what the past few months have held. "It sounds like she's been confabulating," she observes. "Yes!" my brother says. "That's exactly the word!" It occurs to me how foolish we've been, trying to deal with this ourselves. Simply being offered a vocabulary for my mom's behaviors brings enormous relief.

While collecting background, Kathy asks what originally brought my mom to the States. Before I can answer, my brother speaks up. "The idea was never to stay here. Her plan was to go back to India. She just wanted to make some money first."

"What are you talking about?" I interrupt. "She—she said she came here to give her kids opportunities."

My brother regards me with something like pity.

"You know," Kathy intones, "siblings often don't really discuss their parents until something like this happens. I see it quite a bit."

A knock at the door interrupts. By some chance, the doctor assigned to us is an Indian woman I'll call Dr. Singh. She and my mom enter the room, the two of them laughing at some joke in Hindi. I glance at my brother and smile. Camaraderie! Surely this is a good sign.

"So." Dr. Singh sits behind her desk. "I've had a chance to check your mother's vitals and do some baseline cognitive testing. She performed quite well."

My mom straightens up at the mention of her high test scores, chin in the air.

"What concerns me, however, is her weight. Your mom is now eighty-seven pounds. While her score on the MMSE, the Mini–Mental State Exam, puts her—"

"I'm sorry," I interrupt. "Did you say eighty-seven pounds?"

"I did."

I glance at my brother. I glance at Kathy. "That's . . . I mean . . . that's not *good*."

Dr. Singh nods. "Precisely. At her last checkup, she was one hundred pounds. Six months prior to that, she was one-fourteen. Her blood work and labs have all come back normal. . . ."

As Dr. Singh continues, I have to sit on my hands to keep them from shaking. My whole body begins to tremble. The number has rattled me. It is an incomprehensible number—a child's weight.

I look over at her. She's wearing several layers even though it's a warm June day. It's hard to assess her size through the clothing. Have I become so inured to her appearance that I've stopped seeing her?

"I've been dropping off extra meals," my brother interjects.

"We call her," I add. "Once a day, one of us calls to make sure she's eaten."

"Yet her weight has dropped precipitously." Dr. Singh takes off her glasses. "Listen, I don't doubt that you've been trying your best. You're here at this appointment. It isn't easy when you have your own lives—careers, kids."

"I just don't understand how this could have happened. She told us she was eating." My brother rubs a hand across his face.

"I suspect she misremembered." Dr. Singh glances at my mom, whose expression is impassive. Mood Roulette today has yielded Cooperative Mom, who is uncharacteristically quiet. I wonder what's going through her mind.

"She told you she ate, but maybe she was recalling a meal from days before. We have no way of knowing. What is clear is that she needs help."

My mom stirs to life. "I will eat more," she says. "I have been lazy, that is all. No one feels like cooking for just one person. I will make more of an effort. You will see! I will be plump!"

I close my eyes at her familiar phrase.

"We are past that point." Dr. Singh regards me and my brother. "To be frank with you, I am concerned. I cannot in good conscience release your mother to her own care. I don't know if you've had a chance to look into options, but there are some excellent facilities—"

"I'll bring her home with me," I blurt out.

Everyone turns to look at me.

"I work from home," I explain, my voice steadier than I feel. "I'll be able to keep an eye on her. I can cook for her. I'll make sure she eats."

"How long can you do this?" Dr. Singh asks.

"Indefinitely." I think of Noah and Zoe. I don't even know what I'm offering. My brother stares at me in disbelief. "At least until her weight is up," I amend.

"This is a wonderful offer." Dr. Singh beams. "Will you accept?"

My mom smiles vacantly. "I have such wonderful children. I will do whatever they think is best."

I frown. I'm glad she is being agreeable, but I'm annoyed that Kathy and Dr. Singh don't get to see how difficult she can be. It's a bit like taking your car to the mechanic only to not have it make the noise that led you to bring it in.

"Excellent!" Dr. Singh begins making notes in her chart. "Her stomach can't handle large meals, so it's important that you go slow at first. The key is small, frequent portions of high-calorie foods: avocado, peanut butter, ice cream. A daily multivitamin and calcium are also important. I suspect some vitamin deficiency may be in play. . . ."

I take notes on my phone, my thumbs flying, my thoughts a blur. I'm stunned by the thought that I am now in charge of my mother.

"Any questions?" Kathy asks after my mom leaves the room.

"What if she changes her mind?" I ask nervously. "I mean . . . once we're out of here, she isn't going to be as nice. What if she starts yelling?"

"Then let her yell."

My brother clears his throat. "The thing about our mom is that she can be very strong-willed. She's going to demand that she be brought home. She isn't going to remember agreeing to all this."

"Of course she isn't," Kathy agrees.

"So what do I *do*?" I say.

Kathy looks at me. "You're a mom, correct?"

"Yeah."

"Is your kid always cooperative?"

"Well, no, but—"

"Probably screams sometimes, right? Has tantrums?"

"Well, yes, but—"

"It's the same. Don't treat her like she's your mom. Treat her like she's your kid."

I start to object. Kathy doesn't understand.

"Look," she says, tapping her papers into a neat pile, "you hold all the cards here. You drove your mom to this appointment. What's she going to do, walk home?" She chuckles. "Just be sure to lock the doors when you get in the car. That way, she can't jump out."

# 14

The drive to my house is tense.

I keep up a steady stream of banter, my voice artificially cheerful. My mom occasionally murmurs a reply.

She glances out the window as we hit rush hour: sun glinting off metal, cars lurching forward. "What about my things?" she asks as we cross the state border between Connecticut and New York. "If I am coming to your house . . . won't I need my things?"

"Don't worry about it, Mom. We'll figure it out."

She scowls. My reassurances never work on her.

Her mood darkens as we sit in traffic. By the time we pull into my driveway two hours later, she has settled into a ruminative funk. Her face is closed off, shuttered as a boarded-up shop.

Her expression clears when she spots Noah in the doorway. "Oh!" she exclaims. "I didn't know Noah would be home. I thought he would be at work!"

My mom has always loved Noah. She pronounces his name with a subtle *v* in the middle, *No-vah,* which makes me think of a supernova, a bright star. She turns more polite around him, a different part of her clicking into place.

He greets her warmly. (*Of course, honey,* he'd replied when I texted him from the doctor's office. *Bring her home. 87 lbs! That's crazy.*)

Zoe comes tearing around the corner. "Grandma, Grandma! We're so happy you're here!"

"Hello, hello!" she replies, smiling.

I'm braced for awkwardness, but the evening proceeds smoothly. We're actors in a skit, pretending this is a planned visit. We take our cues from my mom, who praises the vegetarian meal I cobble together and declares how wonderful it is to see us. She makes no mention of the doctor's appointment. I wonder if she has forgotten it already.

It's a lovely scene except for her forearm. Resting on the dining table between us, it is smaller than any arm has a right to be—no wider than two pencils. At its widest point, I could encircle it between my thumb and forefinger. As she talks and laughs expansively, I have trouble looking away from it.

After dinner, I make her a peanut butter and banana milkshake. "You made this? It's delicious!" she declares. Because of her memory loss, I'm able to get her to have a little more of it an hour later—small high-calorie portions, as the doctor recommended. She forgets she already had some, finds it delicious anew. "You made this? What is it? It's so good!"

I think to myself that Alzheimer's could lead to starvation or obesity. Short-term memory loss can go either way, causing a person to forget to eat or to eat over and over.

I put Zoe to bed and come downstairs to find Noah and my mom talking in the den. Their conversation is easy, pleasant. Watching them, I feel myself relax.

The den is a windowed space. It is my favorite room in the house, offering a glimpse of the Hudson. The sun sets, the sky softening into a wash of pinks reflected in the water. *Maybe everything will be okay,* I tell myself. *Maybe this won't be so bad.* And then the next day happens.

# 15

✿

"How did I get here?" Her voice is edged with suspicion.

I remind her about the doctor's appointment as I prepare her breakfast.

"So I'm supposed to stay with you?"

"That's the plan."

"That is ridiculous! I cannot live with you. What about my clothes, my house? I do not have any of my things!"

"You need to gain weight, Mom." I place a bowl of maple oatmeal in front of her along with some sliced banana. "That's the deal. I ordered you some new clothes. Your old ones don't fit anyway. Whatever you need, we can get."

She clucks her tongue dismissively. "This is altogether unnecessary. I lost weight out of laziness, that is all. Once I am home I will make more of an effort. You will see! I will be plump!"

"That's what you said last time. You promised you'd gain weight, but you lost a fifth of your body mass in six months." I pause for effect. She doesn't take the bait. "We tried it your way," I continue. "It didn't work."

"Well, you see, the problem is, I have always been a picky eater. Even when I was a girl, this was an issue, my mother always complained . . ."

She has an answer for everything. As we go back and forth,

she remains unflappable while I grow agitated. Logic is of no use. When I tell her she's emaciated, she tells me I'm being dramatic. When I remind her of her doctor's orders, she questions the doctor's credentials.

"Mom, Dr. Singh is a professor at *Yale.*"

"So? Maybe she is a good researcher. That does not make her a good doctor."

"You're skin and bones!"

"In India, plenty of people are skin and bones. Americans are too fat."

It occurs to me that we aren't arguing over food or weight. We're arguing over control.

I think of Kathy, competent Kathy, and draw a deep breath. "Listen, you can argue all you want. It's not going to work. If you want to go home, I'm the one who has to drive you. And I'm not taking you back until your weight is up."

My mom doesn't know about Uber. These days, she wouldn't know how to call a cab. Kathy was right: I hold all the cards. Standing there, I feel triumphant.

"Fine," she says, coolly surveying me. "But if you keep me here, I won't eat." She pushes away her breakfast, having only eaten a few slices of banana.

I stare at her in horror.

"You and your brother want to control me. I know how you are. I will not eat a single bite in this house. What will you do then? You say you care about me. Will you be able to watch me starve?"

"Mom!" I bury my face in my hands. A prisoner's strike! I can't believe she's making threats twelve hours into her stay.

Kathy wanted me to take charge. The truth is, I don't know how. "We'll discuss this later," I mumble.

She smirks.

I climb the stairs to my office, ostensibly to work. I promised my agent I would send her a draft of my second novel by the end of the month. As I open my laptop, I hear my mom wander into the guest room across the hall. I peek my head out and see that she has her purse. "Um, where are you going?"

"I will wait downstairs until you are ready to take me home."

"Mom, I can't. I have work. I have to pick up Zoe after school. And you need to eat!"

"This afternoon, then."

When I check on her a half hour later, she's sitting on the foyer floor.

"What are you doing on the ground like that?"

"I told you. Do you not remember? Maybe you should have *your* memory checked. I will wait here until you can drive me home."

"On the floor? What's the point? At least make yourself comfortable."

She glares at me and turns up her nose.

This is my mother, my brilliant, beautiful mother, but in that moment, her face in a pout, it occurs to me that Kathy was right. She is a child.

A toddler throwing a tantrum eventually gets tired, as any parent will tell you. You can either make yourself miserable trying to reason with the kid or you can make yourself a cup of tea and wait it out.

I choose the latter.

I return to my office. An hour later, I hear her head back to the guest room. I smile, pleased that she has given up. After revising a chapter, I glance at the clock. I'm shocked. It's two o'clock, much later than I thought. My mom hasn't eaten anything since her measly few bites of banana. I knock on the guest room door.

She's sleeping so soundly that she doesn't hear me enter. Lola, no subtle creature, is a veritable marching band as she follows behind me, her tail whacking the door, her paws tapping the hardwood. My mom doesn't stir.

"Mom?" I touch her leg through the blanket.

Disoriented, she mumbles something I can't make out.

"*Mom.*" I shake her leg more firmly.

Her eyes flutter open. They swim in their sockets before rolling back in her head.

Alarmed, I rush to her side of the bed and take her shoulders. "Mom, are you okay?"

She can't bring her eyes into focus. "Tired," she mumbles. She's out again before I can say another word.

I stand there, panicking. Her eyes and their backward roll are something out of a soap opera. Eyes aren't supposed to do that in real life.

Lola looks at me with concern and paws the blanket.

*Maybe she's just tired,* I think. *Maybe she needs rest.*

Except that I know better. I'm making excuses. Fatigue would be one thing. The inability to focus one's eyes is another. She didn't fall asleep so much as lose consciousness.

I reach for my phone to dial 911. It's the right thing to do—I know this—but I can't bring myself to do it. I've heard stories about old people who go into the hospital for something seemingly minor, a broken wrist or a sprained ankle, never to emerge.

I look at her figure beneath the covers. I look at the phone in my hand. I can't let my fear get the better of me. I steel myself.

"*Mom!*" This time I yell the word. I clap my hands loudly. "I need you to wake up. This is an emergency. If you don't wake up, I'm calling an ambulance."

Her eyes fly open.

"Good! Now sit up!"

My voice is the voice of a drill sergeant. I've never taken this tone with my mom. I've never taken this tone with anyone.

She attempts to raise herself. She can barely lift her head. I help prop her against the pillows. "You need to drink this." I hand her a glass of juice from her nightstand.

"Later," she murmurs, her head beginning to droop.

"No! Right now. You hear me? *Right now.*"

If it's possible to drink juice spitefully, she does so.

"You haven't had enough to eat. You're losing consciousness." I feel ridiculous speaking the words. I have no idea what I'm talking about.

She begins to argue. I cut her off.

"Either you eat the snack I bring you or I will have you hospitalized. These are your options. Do you want to be hospitalized?"

She looks down at the blanket and shakes her head.

"Okay. Good."

When I return with a small plate (a KitKat, some crackers, slices of apple, and a small hunk of cheese), thrown together in a rush because I'm worried she'll nod off in my absence, she mutters, "I'll finish it. You don't need to stand over me like that. Just give me five minutes."

I wait in the hall and listen anxiously as she eats. I remember that she once asked me if I wanted to be hospitalized. It is surreal to be asking her the same question.

Emerging from the guest room, she won't meet my eye. She leans heavily on me as we make our way down the stairs, her fingers digging into my arm. The short flight takes us ten minutes.

I assemble another snack for her in the kitchen. She eats it wordlessly, radiating hostility. Anger, I remember once telling the shrink, can be helpful.

I think about how infuriated I was when she refused to visit me in Seattle. She may not have been right in her actions, but she was sure of herself. Maybe it's what I need to be now: not correct, but certain. I can call 911 or go into her room clapping my hands, but I can't stand there indecisively, hemming and hawing. If taking charge causes her to be angry, so be it.

Her first day under my care hasn't exactly been a success. I've threatened her, yelled at her, refused to get medical help when I probably should have, neglected to feed her even though it is my sole task. I engaged with her when I should have ignored her, ignored her when I should have engaged with her. A nurse or aide watching all this would shake their head. I haven't done things perfectly. I haven't even done things well.

Still, as I watch her eat, as I watch color return to her face, I can't help but think that Kathy would be proud.

# 16

That evening when Noah gets home, my mom transforms. Mom Roulette yields the Convivial Houseguest. She cracks jokes at the dinner table, asks Noah warmly about his day. She might as well offer to juggle fruit and make balloon animals.

I watch her a little resentfully. I feel like a stay-at-home mom who's endured a howling infant all day only to have the baby smile beatifically when Dad gets home.

No one would believe me if I recounted our afternoon. Gone is the woman whose eyes rolled back in her head. In a movie, the timing would be implausible, laughing and joking two hours after losing consciousness. My mom sings the praises of my risotto. She sails between moods unfettered. It's not by choice, but it's instructive. I decide to follow her lead and let go of our awful day.

She hasn't been with us for twenty-four hours. It's incomprehensible. I don't know how to keep up with her moods. That night, though, as we linger at the table, the room lit gold by the setting sun, I think that Alzheimer's might bear its own strange gifts.

I suppose it's a strange perk of the disease. Her memory loss frees her. People talk a lot about trying to be "in the moment." Alzheimer's patients have no choice.

Forgiveness has never come easily to me. I have the opposite problem of my mom: a too-sharp memory. It collects things on its points. Her illness offers a startling insight: I don't need to hold on to what my memory hoards.

For the first time, I think that the point of moving my mother in with me isn't just to help her. I might have something to gain as well.

# 17

My mother's arrival presents a big change in our household. It's a bit like having a second child, without the nine months to prepare.

Until this point, home life has been fairly ordered. Zoe is the sort of child who would rather sit with a book than have a play-date. Watching other kids bounce off the walls, she asks why they are behaving that way. She has her own challenges, of course, but they are the challenges of a bookworm. They're my kind of challenges.

My mom is a different story. Each day with her is a roller coaster. She forgets how she came to be in our house and claims she is being held hostage. The next moment she expresses shame at needing help. My fiercely proud mother, who always radiated a palpable authority, who never once cried in front of me, now sobs into my clavicle. Ten minutes later, she is a cheerful bird asking if she can help prepare dinner. "That's why I'm here, you know," she says brightly. "To help you."

What is this tumultuous ride? It is alternately fascinating, entertaining, exhausting. I always knew about Mom Roulette, but I had no idea how much the wheel spun. As I watch her daily ups and downs, as I experience them with her, my irritation fades. Any resentment softens. My poor mother, bouncing from mood to mood.

After three or four days with us, she asks Noah to take her to Target so she can buy almond milk. She delivers a little lecture on organic farming, an episode of *60 Minutes* she once saw involving the USDA, and how she is gluten-free. Noah nods as though this nonsensical speech makes perfect sense. "Clearly," he says, "almond milk is the answer."

Once actually at Target, she decides she wants nothing to do with it. "Almond milk?" she repeats. "Why would I want that?" Instead, she buys an enormous bag of potato chips. After getting home, she points to it and says, "My goodness, you people eat a lot of junk food. You know what I need? Almond milk." I am about to implode when Noah fishes a carton of it out of the shopping bag. "Here," he says with a smile. He bought it at the store by pretending it was for him.

We are learning: how to help her, what we can and can't expect, and how to be more generous versions of ourselves. "Grandma's trying her best," I tell Zoe absently one night after Grandma unloads the dirty dishes from the dishwasher. "Really, that's all she can do." In the moment, I didn't mean it. I said it because it was the right thing to say. The words come back to me in the days that follow.

My mother forces me to practice what I have always claimed to value. Compassion, empathy, patience, kindness. What do they mean if we only ever encounter them in books? How much better to have them alive in my home.

# 18

My mom's been with us for about a week when I glance her way one morning and gasp.

"What?" she says, startled.

"Oh! Um. Nothing. I just remembered something, that's all." For a fiction writer, I make a lousy liar.

I go back to reading the newspaper and fight the urge to stare. The June sunlight streaming through the windows has illuminated her silhouette. Across her chin is a nascent field of white down.

I glance at her surreptitiously. This is the Petite Hairless Wonder. She *can't* have hair on her chin. Yet there it is, not so much hair as dandelion fluff.

Later, I catch her fingers grazing it. A scientist, she has no embarrassment about her body. "I feel hair here. I can't pluck it because of my hand tremor."

"Would you like me to do it for you?" I've been rehearsing the line in my head. I've practiced making it sound casual, as though offering her a glass of water.

She hesitates briefly. "Okay."

I run to grab the tweezers, thrilled that she is letting me do this for her. I have her recline on the couch, her head propped on a pillow.

She closes her eyes. Gently, I lift her chin. The vulnerability of the moment surprises me—her face cradled in my hands, her eyes squeezed shut. My face is inches from hers. Her exhaled air is a soft breeze. My breathing slows to match hers.

I wish that every charge under someone's care, every patient and elderly person and body in distress, could know what I experience in that moment, which is not disgust or repulsion. It is love. You cannot care for a person without thinking of her dignity and beauty, wanting nothing more than to preserve both.

After I finish, she feels her newly smooth skin. Satisfied, she nods. Then her hand flies up and catches mine. "What person does this for another? I can't believe you did this for me." She smiles and releases me.

# 19

How long will my mom stay with us? Will we hire an aide? What about her house in Connecticut? Such questions circle my thoughts. There's one person who finds my lack of answers unnerving. It isn't Noah. It's my brother.

"How long do you think she'll be with you?"

"No idea."

"I mean, I know you can't say *exactly*, but what about ballpark? We need to think about next steps here. I don't want to be in a position where she needs care and we don't have anything in place."

My brother's points are always eminently reasonable. Listening to him, I often find myself thinking that only a moron would disagree.

"If you had to guess," he continues, "like if you *had* to come up with a number—"

"I don't know, okay?" My voice is sharper than I intend it to be. I clear my throat. "Honestly, I can't say. Six months? A year?"

He falls quiet. "I thought you'd say a few more days. A couple of weeks, tops."

"A couple of weeks? She's skeletal!"

"I know that."

"Well, two weeks aren't going to fix it. There was this one day where I couldn't wake her. . . ."

I feel my words failing to land. My brother wants a plan. He seeks a timeline, strategy, next steps, the language borrowed from the business meetings that order his world. He wants to get into the minutiae of insurance, facilities, all of the logistics and arrangements. What I'm feeling has nothing to do with logistics or arrangements.

There is a particular kind of pain when our siblings don't understand us, when they cannot fathom our choices. I sense it on his side: *Six months? A year?* He can't believe I've uttered those words. *Are you guys nuts?* It's what I hear him wanting to say.

I feel it from my side as well. *A couple of weeks, tops.* I can't believe he's said *those* words. *Eighty-seven pounds!* I want to shout, as though repeating the number will make him see it differently.

A long silence passes between us.

"There's no way I could do what you're doing," he finally offers.

I'm not sure how to reply. There is something on the other side of caring for my mother. It's not something I could graph or list, not something I could rationally explain. I am in the middle of something with my mother. What I feel, if I had to put it into words, is the draw of the inexorable. There is unfinished business between us, some work of tending to her and seeing her through. Those are hard words to speak aloud, especially to my brother.

"I can't imagine putting her in a home right now," I say instead.

I think about our Adler appointment, when it came out why she had first come to the States. My mom always told me she had come here to give her kids opportunities. Or, at least, I think she did. Maybe I'd simply assumed it.

This is why I want this time with her. I want to get to know her while I still can. I want to separate the myth from reality, to reconcile the mom I always imagined with the more complicated person I'm just starting to know.

# 20

It is an ongoing battle to find clothes for my mom. The size-four pants I ordered online prove loose, hanging off of her. Her old pants were a size ten. Her whole life, she was a ten. Surely, I thought, the fours would fit.

I order new pants in a size two. They droop. Even the zeroes are baggy. Zoe finds this a hilarious game. "Do pants come in negative numbers?" she asks. Grandma's eyes crinkle with laughter. Going along with the joke, I give her an outfit of Zoe's to try. The sleeves are too short, the leggings more like capris, but otherwise they fit.

"Grandma's wearing my clothes!" Zoe giggles, delighted.

I'm the only one not laughing.

I'm torn between panic and calm. Just like that day by her bedside when I nearly dialed 911, I don't know how scared I should be.

Finally, I make myself look up her BMI. I discover that it's 15.4. Anything below seventeen is used as part of the diagnostic criteria for anorexia, when weight loss has turned so extreme as to require hospitalization. I need such numbers to comprehend what has happened. Like war or abuse, it's difficult to fathom.

Living with her, I understand how she came to be eighty-seven pounds. There is my actual mom, whose actions I observe, and then there is her spokesperson, who specializes in putting those actions in a certain light. My actual mom thinks she's eaten lunch when she hasn't, puts her medication on the counter "for later" and then walks away, forgetting all about it. Her alarmed pillbox was supposed to be foolproof. Dementia makes fools of us all.

My actual mom wants to shower ten minutes after she's showered, to wipe the kitchen counter with a paper towel from the trash, to eat an expired yogurt unearthed from the back of the fridge. I think back to when I prepared meals for her, taking pains to label them in large letters. What good are expiration dates if you don't know the month? I thought I was anticipating her needs, but my assumptions were faulty, clouded by denial. It wouldn't surprise me if she ate food past its prime and became sick.

My mom came to be eighty-seven pounds because when we called, we got the spokesperson on the line. The spokesperson told us about delicious meals and properly taken pills, about a lovely stroll through the neighborhood. The spokesperson strayed so far from the bulls-eye of the truth that she was no longer on the dartboard.

We believed her even though her story didn't square with our observations. We believed her even as her weight dropped and her symptoms worsened. I wanted to endorse whatever version of herself she put forward, the same way she had done for me, the same way she had done for her patients. Her greatest gift was that she believed people. She healed people by taking their side.

Only now does it dawn on me that she never truly believed her patients. To diagnose them, she had to listen critically. The point wasn't to fall for the story. The point was to make the person think she had.

# 21

During the day, I try to set her up with activities so that I can work. I have a fellowship application due, a stack of short stories to read for a fiction contest I'm judging, and there's the matter of my second novel. I give my mom laundry to fold or turn on CNBC and then race up to my office. I take breaks to check on her and make her snacks. I take her on a daily walk, prepare her lunch, look up vegetarian recipes for dinner, and oversee her medication and supplements.

She wanders the house and asks which way the bathroom is. Even after a week, she can't remember her way to the guest room. "Why am I here?" she asks, bewildered.

One morning, I panic because I can't find her. She's outside, seething. She refuses to come in. When I ask why she's mad, she sticks her tongue out at me.

She accuses me of trying to poison her. An hour later she tells me I am the best daughter in the world. She claims my brother is after her money. When she sees Zoe, she turns affectionate. I ricochet between her moods like a ball in a pinball machine.

There is one constant. Each day, without fail, she approaches me with a frightened look in her eyes and tells me she needs to move to an assisted living facility. Now that she is in my care, she doesn't try to be the spokesperson anymore. We are past that.

Zoe's arrival in my life once worked as a mirror, causing me to see myself anew. This is what happens, I think, to my mom. She can no longer see herself through the spokesperson's glossy veneer. She can no longer fool herself into thinking that she is fine. She sees what I see, what neither one of us wanted to admit. I sense how this wounds her but that it is also a relief. She can set down her illusions with me. I can set down my old illusions of her. We can set down our stories together.

# 22

H ow are you?" I ask Noah at night. "Are you okay? Are we
all, you know, *okay*?"

"I'm good."

"Genuinely good, or just-saying-it good?"

"Genuinely good. I thought it'd be stressful having your mom
here. She has her tough moments, but, I don't know, it's been
kind of nice."

"I feel the same way. I wasn't sure if you did."

"It's sweet seeing her with Zoe. And she's already doing so
much better. It's like watching a houseplant come back to life.
Even her eyeballs look better."

It's true, now that he mentions it. "Her eyes . . . when she first
got here, they were sort of . . ."

"Yellow?"

"Yeah. They were. *God*." I think back to how the whites were
neon tinged, like something out of the *Thriller* video. I think
back to when I couldn't sit across the table from her without
having two martinis. Now I'm with her all day and I don't mind.
I don't understand it.

It occurs to me that she and I used to be in a cycle of avoid-
ance. It was painful interacting with her, so I did it less and less.
This made any rewards unlikely.

We interacted in ways that were superficial: small talk, meals, contrived get-togethers. Small talk is a recipe for disaster for Alzheimer's patients because it relies on short-term memory. She repeated herself. I grew frustrated.

Now, our interactions are more organic. We chat while I'm cooking or while we're walking Lola. I don't expect anything of her because I see how hard her daily life is. The miracle is that she manages to be cheerful at all.

Hand someone a screaming baby for five minutes and they might not feel much for the baby. Have that same person watch the baby for an afternoon and they might be reluctant to let the baby go.

When faced with a situation that's driving us crazy, it could be that we need to bring the problem close. It's not a blanket strategy. I wouldn't recommend it for toxic or abusive relationships. Avoiding my dad has worked out pretty well for me. But my relationship with my mom was always different. It was based on love. Limiting our interactions made it difficult to access what we used to share.

I feel better helping her. That's the funny part. She's the one in need of help, yet I feel better providing it. It's odd, but I somehow get the feeling that in the act of caring for her, I'm somehow caring for myself.

# 23

I am brushing Zoe's hair one morning while she tries to squirm out from under me when I hear myself say, "You should be glad! Grandma never used to brush my hair."

"Lucky you," Zoe mutters.

I smile, but it occurs to me that she is right. I brush her hair for my sake. I don't want her to be bullied or to be looked at with pity by her teachers, but those are my fears. What seems a maternal act is at heart a selfish one.

I remember years ago when my mom would visit me in New York, her car loaded up with strange offerings. I knew it was a gesture of love, but those items felt like they had nothing to do with me at all.

Paper towels. Claritin. Wide-spectrum antibiotics. They were the same items she used to pack in a Samsonite suitcase to bring to her parents in India. Their life was comfortable, but they didn't have ready access to Western conveniences.

Maybe my mom brought me items she wished someone had brought her.

Maybe I brush Zoe's hair because I wish someone had done it for me.

Maybe at our most maternal, we aren't mothers at all. We're daughters, reaching back in time for the mothers we wish we'd had and then finding ourselves.

Caretaking offers a chance to atone. My mother didn't drop everything for me when I needed her, but I drop everything for her now. It feels like a do-over, a chance to get things right between us. I'm being the mom she should have been. In doing so, I'm helping us both.

We forget, I think, in the act of caring who is being cared for, that it is not our own hair getting brushed, our own mouths being fed, our own needs being met. We do what wasn't done for us. We hope it will be enough.

# 24

What surprises me in those early weeks is how not-bad our situation is. I'm so braced for awfulness that our daily reality ends up being a pleasant surprise, a kind of "Huh, we're really doing this. And it's *not that bad!*"

There are benefits to having my mom around that I never would have anticipated. If you'd asked me a year ago what I wanted for my family, I might have wishfully rattled off certain desires: to eat more vegetables, to have Zoe be exposed to Marathi, to spend more time together as a family. The thought of these goals felt onerous (who has the time?), but with my mom there, they just happen.

We eat more of a plant-based diet with a vegetarian in the house, mainly because I get tired of cooking different dishes. She speaks in Marathi almost exclusively because Alzheimer's causes language regression. We start playing board games to provide her with mental stimulation: Yahtzee, Rack-O (her favorite, because it's the only one she can manage without help), Uno. There we sit, playing cards after a healthful meal, Grandma making declarations in Marathi that Zoe laughs at shyly. We're a twenty-first-century Rockwellian portrait.

"So, I got a piano," Noah announces one evening.

"Sorry?" I say.

"I didn't want to bother you with everything that's been going on, but I saw an ad online. Some neighbors are getting rid of theirs. I hired a piano tuner to check it out, make sure it's in good shape. We're getting it for next to nothing."

Noah has always been musically inclined. He has perfect pitch. It's a rare trait, said to affect one in ten thousand. Most of his life, he didn't even know he had it until he was in a cab one day, listening to an unfamiliar song, and realized he could somehow "see" the chords. If I tap a wineglass, he can identify the note. Play any song, and he can name the key. For years I've hounded him to pursue it beyond the parlor trick. He's always been drawn to the piano in particular. "One day," he's always said absently.

I laugh. "I love it. How are you finally doing this now?"

He shrugs. "Maybe because now is when I need it."

There is a chance my husband would have taken up piano without his mother-in-law moving in, but honestly, I doubt it. He needed the nudge.

Illness, mortality, the complexity of caring for an ailing loved one: No one would choose to face these scenarios, but in moments of crisis, when we have no choice, we submit. To our surprise, we endure. What choice is there? The not-badness of it is a beautiful thing, a sign that we are stronger than we know.

I thought this was going to be a dark and difficult time for my family, one of strain. It occurs to me that diamonds aren't made voluntarily. What lump of coal would opt for so much time and pressure? It could be that what shapes us against our choosing is what makes us shine.

# 25

Here is a typical day:

My mom wakes up, which might happen anywhere from five A.M. to noon. I'm usually in my office working. I race downstairs to find her standing in the middle of the kitchen in her pajamas, looking bewildered. Once she sees me, she relaxes.

She and I chat for a few minutes in a mix of Marathi and English. I set out her breakfast along with her morning pills. I open the *Times* to an article I think she'll find interesting, a piece on India or the stock market. Then I fly back up to my office to work.

When I hear her coming up the stairs, I zip past her to check that she's taken her medication. She often wants to "rest" after breakfast, from what exertion I cannot say. I set out an outfit for her since she has trouble doing this on her own. "It's nice out— seventy-five," I might tell her. "Do I need a hat?" she'll ask.

Sometimes she showers and changes. Other times she naps on top of the outfit I've laid out. I try to get some work done before lunch, which, depending on when she's woken up, might be an hour after breakfast.

There's a kind of burrito I make for her: cheese, rice, beans, jalapeños, carrots, pickled cabbage, mango, the ingredients prepped on weekends so that all I have to do is assemble them. On a good day, she proclaims the food delicious and tells me to open a restaurant. On bad days, she scowls as she hunches over her plate.

Either way, I race back to work.

In the afternoon I coax her out for a walk. Getting her to leave the house involves a complicated and protracted ritual. She needs a last sip of water, which must have three ice cubes in it, and after the smallest sip, she has to go to the bathroom, after which she needs another last sip of water—and, oh, the ice has already melted! Back to the freezer we go. Lola sighs while watching us, a canine exhalation of despair.

I try not to mind that our walk takes awhile. My mom shuffles along with the classic Alzheimer's gait, her feet pushing rather than lifting. No matter the weather, she sniffles. I don't mean here and there. She sniffles constantly, shockingly, at varying rhythms and volumes and speeds, from delicate aspirations to abruptly violent snorts, a kind of Morse code of the nose: *short short long, short long long.* I once clocked thirty-eight sniffs in sixty seconds.

We stroll for about a mile, sometimes less if she's tired. I miss my brisk walks with Lola. Those walks were when I worked out writing ideas, Lola puffed up with importance at my knee. When my mom is with us, Lola pulls ahead. I don't blame her. She is bored by our slow pace.

When we get back to the house, my mom is exhausted. She returns to her room and stays there. I work until it's time to get Zoe. Soon it's on to dinner prep, Noah sailing through the door, on the phone as he fields a work call, Grandma shuffling into the kitchen. I try to give her a simple task like shelling peas, but she needs to be watched. One night she throws away the peas and hands me the pods.

Zoe's job is to set the table. She co-opts Grandma into the task. "You get the forks, Grandma," she whispers conspiratorially. It is perhaps the best part of my day, watching the two of them. So often with my mom, I tense up, ready to micromanage her. "I know what I'm doing!" she'll snap, opening a peapod. "Mom, the last time you did that, you threw out the peas." "I did?" she says, hurt. "Why would I do that?"

Zoe knows just what to say and just how to say it. She has no expectations. She and Grandma are like siblings or playmates, in on something together, thick as thieves. "The forks are over here!" Zoe calls out if Grandma opens the wrong drawer. It doesn't feel like a correction. Grandma goes over to her with a smile.

I learn from watching them. I learn about kindness and acceptance and patience. I learn to try to meet my mother where she is instead of expecting her to be the person I miss.

# 26

Noah turns to the piano. I turn to the gym. I go on week-nights, after Zoe and Grandma are in bed. Lifting weights is cathartic. It's a way of tending to myself after a day of tending to others.

What surprises me is how different working out now feels. I used to trudge away on the elliptical in a way that felt obligatory and joyless. Now the gym is my sanctuary. My workouts feel like a nearly spiritual practice, a way of honoring the decision to put myself first, even if just for an hour. I've stopped thinking about what I should do. My only goal is to do what I like—which, as it turns out, is lift big, heavy things.

By August, I can squat a hundred and ninety-five pounds. I'm at a respectable five on the pull-up assist.

"So what's your story?" Louis asks during a session.

"What do you mean?"

"I mean, why weren't you an athlete in school? You're an athlete. You get that, right?"

I flush. Lou and I usually don't talk much. We work out with a singularity of focus I relish. We talk only when we need to, usually to discuss form or mechanics.

"You ever try sports? Something happen?"

I shrug.

"Maybe being Indian, that wasn't encouraged?"

"I was on the track team. And the tennis team." I hesitate, unsure how to continue.

"Let me guess. Your dad tried to coach you."

I stare at him. "How did you know?"

"I see it all the time. Parents who yell at their kids. He yell at you?"

I nod.

"Make you do things you hate?"

I nod again.

"Got so that you forgot the joy of the thing, huh?" He shakes his head. "Makes my blood boil, when I see those dads—and it's almost always the dads. Berating kids. Shaming them. Hell, I've seen kids get injured. . . ."

Tears blur my vision as he talks. I remember my dad forcing me to run through shin splints at the local track. I remember him yelling at me to get the ball on the first bounce on the tennis court. I complied because the pain in my legs was better than the pain of his words.

"It's why I don't speak up when something hurts." I don't realize I've said the words aloud until I see Louis's expression.

More than once, after taping up my wrist or knee, Lou has asked why I didn't speak up sooner. He gazes at me now with sympathy.

"Look," I say quickly, "I don't like blaming other people for stuff—"

"No, I get it. Listen, young lady, I want you to do me a favor."

"Okay."

"I want you to go a little easier on yourself when you train. I usually don't tell clients that, but you . . . you're in danger of hurting yourself. I'm proud of your progress, believe me, but I want you to be healthy. Not just fit. *Healthy.* Health is more important than fitness, you know."

Another Lou-ism for the files.

I think about how I've always been so hard on myself. Even though my dad is no longer in my life, his voice still plays in my head.

I begin to repeat Louis's words to myself.

*Be gentle.*

*Go easy on yourself.*

*Health is more important than fitness.*

The words are new for me. They replace a harsher soundtrack.

I start to speak up when something hurts. Lou isn't disappointed or dismissive. He takes me seriously, which helps me take myself seriously.

Listening to my body shouldn't be something new. For nearly forty years I've lived in this body, but whenever it spoke, I turned furious, annoyed that it was asserting itself.

I treated my body the way my dad treated me. I ridiculed it, dismissed it, told it to shut up and fall in line. I didn't want to hear whatever it had to say. I thought my job was to transcend my body. It was uncooperative, forever resisting me, as stubborn and useless as my father once found me.

"How's the body?" Lou asks whenever he sees me. What I really hear is, *How are you? How are you,* really? Louis doesn't want me to be impressive. He wants to know how I feel, the center bulls-eye of the truth, and he doesn't punish me for it.

# 27

The hair on my mom's chin doesn't grow back. I'm in the middle of getting Zoe ready for her first day of second grade when it occurs to me.

My mom has a severe hand tremor. She can't wield tweezers. She has lived with us for more than three months. What sort of hair doesn't grow back?

After dropping Zoe off at school, I look up medical conditions online: thyroid disorders, hormonal imbalances. None of what I read fits. My research eventually takes me to a strange place: a website on eating disorders. I encounter the word *lanugo*, which I remember from when Zoe was born. It's the fine hair that coats newborns. Apparently it sprouts in the later stages of starvation and takes the appearance of down. Dandelion fluff.

I swallow. I type "signs of starvation body shutting down" in the search bar. A medical website pops up. Jaundiced eyes. Disorientation. Moodiness. Fatigue. Intolerance of cold. The development of fine hair or lanugo. The last is the body's attempt to keep itself warm.

My mother was so emaciated that her body had started to grow its own blanket.

I think back to her disoriented state, how she couldn't find her way to the bathroom. I remember her sticking her tongue out at me and accusing me of poisoning her. I blamed her

Alzheimer's. I thought she was going through a phase that was especially bad, Mood Roulette failing to work in my favor.

It's funny what we tell ourselves when life doesn't add up. The twig of a forearm or the expansive laughter of its owner. Neon yellow eyes or a willful tantrum. We ignore one and heed the other. We do this in the name of coherence, dismissing the evidence before us. If she could stage a hunger strike and crack jokes with Zoe the same day, she couldn't be *that* bad. This was what I told myself. She didn't have a spokesperson anymore, so I supplied one for her.

That first afternoon when she couldn't focus her eyes, I nearly dialed 911. I stopped myself. . . . Why? Not because she wasn't that bad, but because I couldn't bear the thought of her being hospitalized.

Her body had been speaking, but I didn't want to listen.

Was she close to death that day? It seems preposterous.

*Do you want to be hospitalized?* I asked her.

It was the same question she had once asked me.

How close was she to death?

How close was I?

These questions don't give way to easy answers. Facts are subject to endless interpretation. Alzheimer's, vitamin deficiency, starvation: Where does one end and the other begin? Suicidal ideation: What is a desperate request for help versus idle talk? When is someone in danger?

Neither my mom nor I reacted as we should have. When I was a suicidal teen, she watched me play piano. When she lost consciousness, I fixed her a snack. Our reactions were woefully inadequate. They were responses born of fear.

Caretakers are supposed to be objective. The more you love your charge, the less likely this is. Caregiving and parenthood aren't singular activities, after all, but a mix. You worry, assist, feed, clean up after, encourage, observe. The more good you see, the more filled up you feel. "She can't be that bad" is a way of saying "I'm not that bad." "She's doing okay" means "I'm doing okay."

I don't see my mother clearly. I pride myself on my care of her, the fact that her eyes are now clear and bright, her moods less erratic, her weight healthy. I want to believe she's thriving. Is it true?

"You are going to be fine," she told me when I was depressed. She must have said it for her sake as much as for mine. Love blinds the caregiver to danger. To acknowledge danger is to acknowledge the possibility of loss.

# 28

As I adjust to my mother's needs, I realize she will never again live alone. It should have been obvious right away, but the realization comes haltingly, fumblingly, a slow-to-dawn "Oh."

I tell my brother that we should sell her house. She frets about it, worried she forgot to lock the doors or turn off the oven.

My brother resists. "If we sell it, we won't have a plan B. She'll either have to live with you or be in a facility."

"Right. I think that's where we are."

"Yeah, but if you guys were to travel . . . I mean, right now, we could do something where she stays at her place and I check on her, bring her food . . ."

"That's how she got to be eighty-seven pounds!"

"Presumably her weight can't drop too much if you're on vacation."

I sigh. "Presumably" is the sort of word my brother uses. He's a problem solver. He isn't terribly moved by emotions or heartstrings, isn't always sensitive to the subtleties of a situation, the same subtleties that work overtime on me. This is not to say he's unkind. He is deeply generous and caring. He just doesn't want to take care of our mom in his house.

I get it. I don't blame him. I was the one who brought her home with me, but the decision has ramifications for him.

Relationships vary. I'm not one to judge. I haven't spoken to my dad in years. Keeping him out of my life hasn't required much effort, but it has been a choice.

In September, my brother agrees to list our mom's house on the condition that we make "arrangements" should Noah and I ever need an extended break. I agree without wanting to think about what those *arrangements* would be. My brother hires a real estate broker, donates my mom's furniture, and makes quick work of her belongings. This is how he "adds value," to use his sort of phrase.

"Can't your brother watch your mom for a month or two?" friends ask. I feel protective of his boundaries, of whatever he has decided, maybe because I know how difficult such boundaries are to establish. "That's not an option," I reply.

I'm estranged from my dad. My mom is estranged from herself. I don't want to lose my brother.

He still sees my dad on occasion. I trust that he will respect my boundaries with my dad just as I respect his boundaries with my mom. So often, siblings are inverses, yin and yang. We make no sense to one another. What works for one doesn't work for the other, nor should we expect it to.

# 29

There's no way I could do that."

"You guys are saints."

"God bless your family."

The compliments that pour in from friends and neighbors as I share the news that my mom has moved in with us are nice but off-putting. They don't describe my reality.

It reminds me of when Zoe was an infant and strangers accosted me. "Isn't this time just the *best*?" people would remark. "Doesn't it just *fly*?" Battling postpartum depression, I was in no position to agree.

"Really," I insist now, "I'm enjoying this time with my mom." Friends raise their eyebrows, dubious. They ask how I'm coping. They ask if I have any support. Where were these questions when I became a new mother?

It's possible that we should switch around what we say, tell new moms that they're angels. "I don't know how you're doing it." "Do you have enough support?" "My God," we should say with a shudder, "what you're doing is amazing."

To caretakers of aging parents, we might try, "Isn't this time with them the *best*?" Because when I'm walking Lola with my mom, when I watch her and Zoe play cards, it occurs to me how lucky I am—to have a flexible career that enables me to care for her, to have a house with a spare room, to have a spouse who welcomes the arrangement.

I never imagined that caring for an elderly parent could be rewarding, perhaps because it's a departure from conventional living arrangements in this country. The American way is supposed to be better. It's what I always believed. Caring for my mom, I appreciate the very different model of family life that exists in countries like India where multigenerational homes abound. When young and old cohabitate, people in need of support can actually get it.

My *agi* in Bombay never lived in a nursing home, despite having had dementia. My brother's stories of her strike me as remarkably peopled, filled with cousins and relations and neighbors. Not everyone was wonderful to *Agi*, not everyone knew how to help, but her care never fell to one person—just as my brother's care as a boy was distributed among relatives. It makes me realize how lonely modern American households are.

Rewarding though caretaking can be, it has its tough moments. My friends tell me I'm doing a good deed, but I don't live with their perceptions. The roof leaks. The washing machine breaks. Zoe comes down with a high fever the same week my fellowship application is due. I want there to be a correlation between good deeds and real life. There is no karma as far as the roof is concerned. Zoe has glassy eyes and a temperature of 103.8°. I tend to her, tend to Grandma, look into roof repair, cook vegetarian dishes, watch the laundry pile up, stay up all night to work on my fellowship deadline. It feels like too much. It is. It's life.

But now, unlike in Seattle, I don't feel panicky. All that time as a new mother when I felt overburdened functioned like my time in the gym. It strengthened me. I know now how much I can carry.

# 30

One afternoon, while making Grandma and Zoe after-school smoothies, I overhear them talking. Zoe tells Grandma all sorts of things she doesn't tell me. I'm astonished.

I wonder in that moment how well I listen to my daughter, if I really invite her confidence. Too often when with her, I'm in the middle of doing something else (cooking, cleaning, helping Grandma). When she talks, I'm on the lookout for warning signs—if she's being bullied, if she's understimulated, overstimulated, if there is more as a parent that I need to *do*.

A child doesn't know how to edit a story or how to get to the point. Sometimes there is no point at all, just a story she would like to share, words she would like to say aloud, for reasons she herself may not understand.

Grandma receives these words. Grandma isn't in the middle of cooking dinner or on deadline. She listens and nods. I look on, amazed. To me, Zoe shrugs and says, "School was good." With Grandma, she goes on at length about recess and music and gym class.

It occurs to me that I didn't confide in my mom as a girl. The magic door came much later—after I had moved out. As my mom disengaged from my dad, as her load lessened, she had more time for me.

I love Zoe's unique bond with her grandmother, but watching the two of them is hard. I can't help but be jealous. It also makes me wonder how available I am to my daughter when I am spread so thin.

# 31

✿

One morning, my mom makes herself a cup of tea. I am ecstatic. After weeks of showing her how ("This is where we keep the spoons"; "This is how to use the kettle"), weeks during which I'm not sure she retains a thing (after a month, she still can't find the mugs), weeks during which I wonder why I bother, watching her finally do it is as jubilant a moment as when Zoe took her first steps. When I text Noah the news (*She made her own tea!!!!*), he can't believe it.

The episode also drives home our reality.

"You made yourself tea!" I crow.

"I did?" she replies blankly.

She doesn't remember making it, can't say how the still-warm mug came to be in her hands. The accomplishment marks a ceiling in an ever-shrinking space.

A woman who once saved lives can now do no more than make tea. It's bittersweet, like building sandcastles on the shore. All that work speaks to its pending erasure.

The episode with the tea helps me grasp my situation. I can't fathom my mother's disease, can't wrap my mind around what it and our living arrangement mean, but a small anecdote involving tea is manageable. It gives me a story, a way to explain (to others and to myself) the ineffable. It gives me a few lines when the rest of the tale is out of reach.

Alzheimer's is devastating because it annihilates one's story. It vacuums it up. Even the name feels greedy to me. What gets me is the apostrophe, that possessive little hook. It drags your loved one away from you. My mom no longer belongs to me. She belongs to her illness.

My time with her is a way of countering that apostrophe. The episode with the tea, in giving me a story, allows me to stake a claim on her. The magnitude of the ocean can be overwhelming, but a sandcastle, however fleetingly, defies that power. Its beauty is more poignant for its brevity.

I can't comprehend what is coming for my mom, the tidal wave of loss, but in the meantime, we have this, tea together in the kitchen. Even if she doesn't remember it, I will. It is enough to get me through the next day, and the next.

# 32

The most difficult days for me aren't when my mom throws tantrums or yells. I am braced for those. The hardest days come from the minor hassles of living with someone who doesn't have her wits about her.

She steals my underwear.

She adds twenty minutes to the time it takes to leave the house.

She hums off-key, which drives Noah crazy.

Then there is the matter of her mouth guard.

She carries it from her bedroom to the bathroom to disinfect it. Because of her memory loss, she does this four, five, six times a day. She refuses to leave it in the bathroom, insists on ferrying it back and forth. The little plastic tray gets filled to the brim with a green medicinal solution. Gripped between her shaking hands, it makes its perilous journey across the hall. Liquid sloshes onto the hardwood floor. I follow behind like a somme-lier, dabbing, dabbing, dabbing, thinking about the life I lead and if the not-badness is so wondrous after all.

# 33

If I'm going to stay here, I need to pay rent."

"Mom, we're not charging you rent."

"But I need to contribute!"

"Noah and I are happy to do this."

"You say that now because I have only been here a few weeks. How will you feel when it becomes a few months?"

It's already been a few months, but I don't correct her. Instead I shrug and say, "We'll talk about it when the time comes."

My mom has become even more fixated on money, though her Alzheimer's twists her perceptions. "I gave your brother so much money. He took advantage!" She slipped him a twenty on occasion for food. Her distorted memory multiplies the twenties into thousands of dollars. She fires off emails to him in the middle of the night accusing him of stealing from her. It's why I won't accept a dime. I don't want her turning on me.

"If you won't let me pay rent, at least let me help around the house. Vacuum, dust. You know how I love to clean."

I hesitate. My housekeeping efforts have lagged since leaving Seattle. Truthfully, I could use the help.

I set her up with a duster. She looks pleased to have a task. When I peek downstairs an hour later, she's still at it, humming away. Who cares if she's dusted the same silver frame five times? It's spotless; I'm able to get some work done. I'm thrilled.

The next day I set her up with the duster in another room. The day after that I give her some paper towels and Windex for the French doors, the glass a mosaic of smudge marks from Lola's inquisitive snout. My mom polishes the glass until it shines. "I should have been a maid! Look at how spotless!" she declares proudly.

That same afternoon she asks me to fix her iPad. I turn it on to find a message to a distant cousin in mid-composition. *Please send help. My daughter is abusing me. She is taking advantage! I am a slave here.* I look at my mom, stunned, before hastily closing the window. I reestablish Wi-Fi.

*Whoosh* goes the outgoing message.

When my mom asks the next day what she can do, I tell her not to worry about it. I won't take her money and I won't ask her to do chores. I want her story with us to be a happy one, a story so good that she has no complaints.

# 34

By October, she has settled in. Her house has sold. We've brought her favorite items back for her. She's no longer in the guest room but *her* room. She stops asking if she can contribute to household expenses.

Still, she is a fountain of worries. She asks about the real estate broker's commission and her furniture. Her questions are self-protective. She doesn't want to know if the sale of her house presented a hassle. She wants assurance that she was compensated properly. "It's ridiculous!" I fume to my brother. "You'd think she could be a little grateful! Instead she wants to make sure we aren't scamming her."

Meanwhile, her nest egg sits untouched. She was a doctor who lived modestly. There were no vacations or shopping sprees. She wore clothes that her kids left behind, including my brother's gray Members Only jacket from 1986, which, in a fit of exasperation, I donated a few years ago. She still asks about it. "Whatever happened to that nice gray jacket?"

She didn't have a mortgage. Her house was paid for in cash. A modest bungalow surrounded by identical bungalows, it depressed me, not because it was so awful but because of what it represented: thrift over pleasure. She never liked the house. She liked the price.

Her one splurge was with long-term life insurance. She got

the Cadillac of plans. When it came to life, she was a miser, but for death she spent like a king.

All her life, she saved for a rainy day. She was so busy preparing for rain that she never stopped to feel the sun. You'd think her fastidious preparations would mean she could finally relax, but there is no umbrella big enough for her.

At night, I hear the rustle of papers: Fidelity statements and Ameritrade printouts being shuffled and redealt as she fans them across her bed. Her game of financial solitaire brings her no pleasure. She makes obsessive notes in the margins. With her hand tremor, the notes are scarcely legible. They have a frantic quality, as though they were written while being electrocuted.

In the initial chaotic blur of tending to her, I didn't think about money. She had needs. I addressed them. I bought clothes, furniture, reading glasses, orthopedic slippers, anything to make her more comfortable. Noah and I didn't mind, but after a while, especially now that she's comfortable, our patience wears thin.

She eats the fancy imported burrata but claims to be lactose intolerant when we're at the cheese shop. She devours the bananas I've been saving to make Zoe's favorite muffins but refuses to buy bananas when I take her to the store.

She operates on her own schedule, waking at noon, still in her pajamas at dinner. She leaves rooms without turning off the lights, accepts the food I cook without a word of thanks, makes lists of items she would like me to procure (sneakers, sweaters, socks, bras). She ignores the books I get her from the library, the YouTube videos I find of Marathi songs. Music, everyone tells me, can bring Alzheimer's patients joy. Try telling that to my mom. Her only pastime as such is to pore over financial statements, counting and recounting her money, making various cryptic notes to ensure it's all there.

Is the behavior an anomaly? What is the Alzheimer's and what is her?

I've always seen my mom through the lens of her work: a prized psychiatrist who was a champion of her patients. I made this her defining trait because of what it meant for me. By turning up the volume on her compassion, I gave it to myself, a kind of vicarious empathy. She was on her patients' side. Therefore, she was on mine.

Truthfully, my mom wasn't a terribly empathetic person. "It's just the medication," she said whenever patients complimented her. I thought she was being modest. She was being sincere.

When a person shows you who she is, you should believe her, yet I bent over backward to see otherwise. Focused on the fantasy of a devoted mother, I chose to ignore so much.

She could be aloof. She never gave money to the homeless or to charity. She tipped terribly and was curt to strangers. She refused to make skin contact when paying someone. This last trait pained me, for while I could always add dollar bills to restaurant tabletops or outstretched paper cups on sidewalks, while I could murmur kindnesses on her behalf, there was nothing to be done in that awful moment of a transaction. She placed cash or credit card on the counter, pointedly ignoring the person's hand. Maybe this was because of her Brahmin upbringing and the caste system's reprehensible view of "Untouchables," but she made the choice to behave that way even after decades in this country. When there wasn't an available neutral surface, she held the bills as far from the recipient's fingers as possible. I felt the person's defeat, the way they became smaller in that moment.

To her, I was an anomaly. I donated and volunteered, overtipped and overthanked. I embarrassed her for my lack of reserve. Once, I admonished my mom about how much service people rely on tips. "Oh!" she said. That was all. One word followed by ponderous silence, as though being shown a piece of furniture it was too late to return.

She mostly kept her judgments to herself, but sometimes they slipped out. "Wash your hands when you leave that AIDS place," she advised when I volunteered at a hospice in high school. "And put your clothes straight into the laundry. Better to be safe with those people."

*Those people.* The words caused me to hang up on her. They didn't match the mom in my head, the one who had boundless sympathy for others.

It's not who I wanted my mom to be, but it's who she was: haughty, self-centered, prejudiced, and, in her own cheap way, a snob. Seeing her plainly means losing the idealized version of her that has existed in my head.

# 35

As my mother and I drop our pretenses, I find that I can ask her anything. "If your plan all along was to go back to India, why did you say you'd come to the States to give your kids opportunities?" I ask. "I did not want to tell you it was an accident," she replies bashfully.

I voice all the nagging questions I had as a kid. Did Ruby really follow her home without a leash? "Probably a servant carried her," she admits. What about giving birth? Did it really not hurt? She chuckles. "If I do not remember any pain, probably I had an epidural."

One day, it occurs to me to ask the biggest question of all. "Mom," I say slowly, "how did you know you wanted to be a psychiatrist?"

"I didn't," she answers right away. "I wanted to be an OB-GYN."

She explains that she suffered from postural hypotension, meaning she couldn't stand for long periods of time without getting dizzy—a deal-breaker for performing C-sections. With her dream job ruled out, she settled for psychiatry. "That way I could sit in a chair," she says.

For the next several days, I am in a state of shock. A neighbor could confess to committing murder, and all I would think about was my mom's desire to be an obstetrician.

"Psychiatry did not appeal to me at all," she admits. "So many problems! Listening to people can be very boring, you know. At least babies are a source of happiness."

It is the last straw, the final puzzle piece that makes me realize how much I deluded myself where she was concerned. The crux of her identity was an accident! She became a psychiatrist out of a desire to be seated!

She hadn't planned for me all along. Her trajectory wasn't a straight line.

"I wonder sometimes why I did not go back to India," she remarks one morning over tea. "Staying in this country, you know. It just . . . happened." What a surprise it would have been to hear this as a girl, to know that my mother was someone to whom things happened, that this was permissible.

She wanted to give me the illusion that she had known what she was doing. It was an illusion I once sought to give my daughter as well. That was the goal of the letters I wrote when pregnant: *Look at how loved you are! Look at how I thought of you all along!* Except, as I discovered, the letters were for my sake, a way of forging my way into my new role.

I deluded myself where my mother was concerned. I let her delude me, too. But this is not to say that those illusions were meaningless. My mom's old stories may have been riddled with untruths (*Daycare did not exist back then!*), plagued by a suspicious lack of detail, but they defined her. They weren't necessarily true to events, but they were true to her. As a writer, I should have known better. I of all people should have understood that a story needn't be accurate in order to be true.

Now that the illusions have been stripped away, I miss my mythic mom. I suspect she misses her, too.

I've been taking care of her physical needs, but who has she become under my care? She has lost her former stature. She is stronger, able to take the stairs without help, able to go on longer walks, but she lacks her old haughtiness. Maybe it doesn't matter whether our stories are true or false. What matters is that they are ours.

# 36

"I want to move back to New Jersey," she announces one day.

"New Jersey?" I repeat. "Mom, what are you talking about?"

"I can't stay with you forever."

"But . . . you can't live on your own."

"I know that. There are nursing homes in New Jersey. Indian ones! Places with Indian cuisine and cinema, everything in our language."

"You mean places that specialize in Marathi?"

"Or Hindi! I speak many languages, you know. Punjabi, Gujarati. That way I can eat food I like." She pokes sullenly at the pasta with porcini mushrooms I've made for dinner, the same dish that's previously earned high praise.

I'm about to argue that New Jersey is too far away, that if anything were to happen, I wouldn't be around to help. Then I remind myself that the point isn't to believe her. The point is to make her feel heard. "Hmm," I say. "Well, that's certainly an option."

Because I don't shoot her down, she begins to talk about New Jersey more and more. She rhapsodizes about it. "When I lived in New Jersey, it was the happiest time of my life. I had my cousins and friends around me. So many people!"

I bite back my retort. No matter that she went years without seeing her cousins, that she stopped talking to many of them after her divorce, convinced they disapproved of her. No matter that her happy associations with that time are probably from her post-divorce freedom. No matter that New Jersey is a whole state and that she inhabited one small corner of it. She is spinning a tale, the details irrelevant.

Her stories grow more fantastic. She tells me she used to go for walks and see "dozens and dozens of Indian people." This is demonstrably false. She lived in a gated community that was overwhelmingly white, with neighbors named Joan and Bob. "I used to walk to Indian restaurants!" she says dreamily. "Everyone said hello!"

At night I fume to Noah about this mythos of New Jersey: Indian Sesame Street, a place of boundless friends and snacks. "Maybe Elmo was there with a platter of samosas," I grumble.

Yet no matter how much I seethe, no matter how ridiculous her tales, I don't correct her. I don't remind her about Joan and Bob. I don't point out that the closest Indian restaurant was miles away. "That sounds nice, Mom," I say instead.

"Yes," she says, sighing. "It was."

I know what stories can mean—especially the ones that aren't true.

# 37

In the sixth grade, my class went on an overnight field trip.
Years later I can't remember the name of my teacher, but I
remember the name of that place: Frost Valley. The name itself
seemed to sparkle with anticipation.

I have no idea why we went. I can't imagine the trip's intended
purpose. I only know that I was utterly unprepared for it. I had
never been to a friend's house for dinner, let alone attended a
sleepover. "I'm going to have to use a fork!" I said to my mom.
She smiled and said, "My goodness, that's right." I was used to
eating meals by hand.

The Indian system is a sensible one: The right hand scoops up
food while the left remains unsullied for one's drinking glass
and serving utensils. My sandwich at school didn't challenge
this, nor did the occasional slice of pizza at a birthday party.
Frost Valley was probably designed to teach us about nature and
teamwork, but as far as I was concerned, it was a test in Ameri-
canness. I had no reason to think I'd pass.

On the bus, kids were amped up—away from parents, in a
new setting, able to ogle crushes. The thought of bunk beds and
cutlery didn't seem to terrify anyone but me. As the bus climbed
steep and snowy hills, rumors spread about bears and ghosts,
the boys trying to make the girls squeal. I observed it all with a
sinking feeling.

School, a place of books and tests and raised hands, was an ecosystem where I thrived. I don't know where I got my confidence from—in retrospect, it seems deluded—but I held my head high. I wasn't a rose, an object of beauty and admiration, but I had a sharp tongue and knew how to wield it, which counts for something in the sixth grade. I suppose I was like a Venus flytrap: slightly feared and duly respected.

As the bus ascended, my usual confidence fell away. It wasn't coming with me into those mountains.

That very afternoon we embarked on our first activity: snowshoeing. Other kids had snow pants and ski parkas with colorful tags. I didn't have any of that stuff.

My mom was too preoccupied to think about the trip. I'd studied the list my school provided with its strange items (long johns, wool socks). I'd improvised as best as I could. When my mom, eyeing my duffel, asked, "So you have everything you need?" what choice did I have but to say yes?

Snow crept into my cotton socks. It dampened my tennis shoes. Other kids were having a blast—throwing snowballs, laughing—while I shivered. When I tripped and fell, Mike Tumo came bounding over to me.

Mike Tumo and I had an unlikely friendship, jock and nerd, honed over months of sitting next to each other in homeroom because that was where the alphabet had placed us. "You okay?" he said. His cheeks were pink from running. His brown eyes showed concern. I shook my head.

Soon a teacher was helping me up and leading me inside. What a relief, to be away from everyone. "Are you in pain?" the teacher asked.

"I'm okay."

"Do you want to try going back out?"

"No! I just . . . um . . . it hurts when I move."

I wasn't old enough to know how to properly fake an injury. I didn't want to cause alarm, but I didn't know how to explain the real problem. I didn't have the right gear or the right parents. What should have been a fun adventure felt hopeless. Not knowing how to say any of this, I made indeterminate noises when the teacher probed my knee.

"It doesn't look swollen," he said, looking worried. "I doubt it's a fracture. Maybe it's just a sprain?"

"Yes!" I said. "You know, I sprained it before."

"You did?"

"Um, yeah. A couple of months ago."

"And you saw a doctor? And it felt like this?"

I nodded fervently.

That poor man. He no doubt feared ramifications: furious parents, the threat of a lawsuit. I wanted to tell him that my parents weren't like that. They'd never side against a teacher. I wanted to tell him not to worry, that I just wanted to be left alone, but kids can't say what they really want. They'll only get talked out of it.

Round and round the Ace bandage went. Crutches were procured. "This is much better," I said, sitting by the windows under a blanket. "Really, this helps. Thank you."

On crutches, I felt more capable. I could participate in activities I liked—namely, ones that involved sitting around and talking. I'm great at sitting around and talking.

I was excused from what terrified me: strange American games, outdoor activities. I didn't know how to explain why I couldn't do that stuff. I didn't want to tell anyone about how I couldn't ask my parents for snow boots, for example. People would assume we couldn't afford them.

My brother was in college. I didn't think to call him for advice, any more than it would have occurred to me to ask the

Frost Valley staff for a spare winter coat. I only knew that those crutches saved me. They kept me from having to stutter through a story I didn't know how to tell. Those crutches were my crutch.

From my seated perch, I could watch everyone. I noticed that Mike Tumo, though pretending to flirt with Nicole, the way all the boys were, was really watching Colleen. I'd have to ask him about that later. I noticed that two of the teachers kept looking at each other shyly, especially during the barn dance. I noticed all kinds of things from my chair. I found that I liked noticing things.

When I got home, my mom wasn't too concerned about my knee. I'm sure she took a look at it at some point. Maybe she even took me to the doctor. What I remember is that she believed me. When I told her it was getting better, she said, "Okay."

My dad was another matter. He eyed me suspiciously. "Probably you just want the attention," he said. "Girls always want attention."

I didn't. I hated having everyone watch me hobble through the lunchroom. Crutches, if you've never had them, aren't much fun. My armpits grew tender. My triceps ached. I didn't want to be the object of scrutiny. I'd just wanted to be out of the snow that first day, and then I felt obligated to carry on with the charade.

My father wasn't content to let me slide. He kept trying to catch me out. "I thought it was your left knee," he'd say.

"No. It's my right."

"Mom said you can't bend it?"

"Yeah."

"You must be getting lots of sympathy at school, eh?"

"Not really."

I figured I'd give it a day or two. If I could make it to the weekend, I could show up to school on Monday crutch-free.

Friday morning: the sound of my doorknob turning at dawn. Some instinct told me to keep still. I opened my eyes very slightly and saw my father enter the room.

He stood at the foot of my bed for a long time. I kept my breathing steady, did the best possible semblance of someone fast asleep. He lifted the covers at the bottom of the bed and felt around with his hand.

My heart pounded as he grasped my foot, but I didn't react. I didn't sit up and say, "What on earth are you doing?" He could have done anything to me in that moment and I wouldn't have said a word. My terror was too great.

He lifted my right leg in the air and tried to bend it. I kept it rigid. He tried harder. My knee didn't budge. He put it down and lifted the other leg, the healthy one. That one I allowed him to bend freely, which he did several times in a row. He sighed and left.

That night at dinner, he cleared his throat. "I went into your room this morning when you were asleep," he said.

I looked up and feigned innocence. "You did?" I said, blinking.

"I lifted your right leg, the so-called injured one. And you know what? It bent just fine." He took a bite of his food.

I stared at him in disbelief. I knew I'd kept that knee locked. I remembered his defeated sigh.

"A knee that works when you're asleep and doesn't work when you're awake . . . that's kind of funny, eh?" He glanced at my mom.

She didn't respond. He often tried to build little cases against me. She mostly ignored him.

"So what do you have to say about that?" he pressed.

I looked down at my plate. I wanted to tell him that he was lying, that I'd been awake the whole time. I could have recounted the whole thing—how he'd stood over my bed, how he'd waited, wanting to be sure I was asleep. Did he really think I'd slept through his calisthenics?

I wanted to call him out, but I couldn't. Partly, I was scared. Contradicting my father was a fool's errand. He'd ask why I pretended to be asleep, accuse me of lying, start yelling at me, and then I'd curse myself for having spoken.

Mainly, though, I felt something that I had never felt before: pity. Confronting him felt cruel. He needed the lie. I understood this. I didn't respect him, but I respected his story.

"It's weird, I guess," I said, shrugging.

My mom shot me a small smile.

I stayed on the crutches for an extra week. Fighting with him was never fun, but watching him fume and mutter to himself, unable to wrest my story from me—that was a sort of win.

A story is something no one can take from you. However much he dominated our house, our lives, even my body, what I could and couldn't do with it, that story was something even he couldn't touch.

# 38

An ongoing struggle for me is how to heed Louis's advice and ease up at the gym. My dad's voice persists in my head, telling me I am worthless and weak. One night I ignore the tightness in my legs while doing box jumps and feel my calf buckle with an audible *pop*. It turns out I've torn the muscle.

By the time I get home, I can't put weight on the leg. Noah retrieves a pair of crutches from the garage.

The next morning when my mom spots me waylaid on the couch, ice pack on my leg, she pauses only briefly before shuffling off to the kitchen.

She doesn't ask Noah what happened. After breakfast, she sits down next to me. "How are you feeling?" she asks.

It's been said that Alzheimer's is similar to improvisational theater. My mom doesn't ask what happened because, as far as she knows, I've been on crutches for days. Her questions over the next few weeks are carefully phrased. "How does it feel?" "Does it hurt?" She won't specify a body part, won't ask about my leg, because for all she knows it could be a foot or a hip. In the game of improv, my mother is an ace.

She was trained in assessing Alzheimer's, after all. She was the one who once determined if a patient needed to be institutionalized. She knows all the tricks. Prideful by nature, she isn't the type to admit ignorance. Never would she say, "I'm sorry—

I can't remember why you're on crutches. What happened?" She won't apologize or admit shortcomings. She assumes control. "How are you feeling?" She plays doctor even though she's the patient.

Each morning I see the series of reactions pass over her features: the initial surprise at my crutches, then her quick recovery and shrewd calculation as she selects the words that won't give her away. "How does it feel?" "Are you in pain?"

Crutches once taught me about the importance of stories. Now they strip me of one. I've been telling myself that my mom is flourishing under my care, that she's lucky to stay with us. I haven't been building her independence, though. I've been building her reliance on me.

*Too much strength can be its own weakness,* Louis once told me. I finally see what he meant. I am overcompensating for my mother, playing too large a role in her life. I have become her crutch.

My adolescent discovery with crutches was an exhilarating one. This one depresses me. I realize how much I've been propping her up. My mother is worse than I thought.

# 39

"Her condition isn't in line with her tests." This is how Dr. Singh puts it.

Every time we go to Adler, driving up to Connecticut for the appointment, my mom takes something called the Mini–Mental State Examination. It's a simple assessment of cognitive function. The highest possible score is a thirty. Anything below a twenty-four is considered a red flag. My mom scores in the high teens.

"I'm not sure I understand," I say. "Her score . . . you feel it isn't an accurate reflection of her dementia?"

"Perhaps she does well because she used to administer the test. Or she might just be a good test taker. Whatever the reason, her symptoms don't correlate."

"Which symptoms do you mean?"

"Hiding objects in strange places. Hoarding food. Decreased hygiene. Sleeping more. You've mentioned all of these."

It's funny. Hearing my mom's behaviors repeated back to me changes them somehow. The anecdotal turns clinical.

Recently, my mom has been secreting away her purse and then, in a panic, saying she lost it. Once I found it in the hamper. Another time it was under her pillow.

She stashes chocolate in her room, including Zoe's Halloween candy. This is the same woman who claims to dislike sweets.

I open her dresser drawers to put her laundry away and find handfuls of truffles, stacks of chocolate bars. She amasses chocolate like gold in wartime.

She fights me if I try to wash her sheets. I invent clever ways to lure her out of the room so that I can strip her bed.

This is the person I know and live with. I see her differently through Dr. Singh's eyes. The daily occurrences that cause me to groan or laugh aren't quirks. Dr. Singh sees them for what they are: the classic behaviors of dementia.

"You also mentioned that she's started to follow you."

I feel bad for having shared this, as though keeping it to myself would mean it wasn't happening. "Yeah, she's been tailing me through the house. She'll follow me from room to room. Sometimes I come out of the bathroom and she's right there, waiting."

"We call that shadowing. I'll have Kathy give you some reading material." Dr. Singh pauses. "Your mother's behavior . . . it usually correlates with a cognitive score of twelve or thirteen. You should prepare yourself. She might start turning on you."

"Turning on me how?"

"She might criticize you as a parent. She could make painful accusations."

"She's already done those things," I say quietly.

"Then you should be prepared for those behaviors to escalate. I wish I had better news. I'm sorry to say it, but your mom's condition has advanced."

# 40

Mommy, why did Grandma say that thing about the sour cream?" Zoe asks one night as I tuck her in.

It was a tough evening: the first time my daughter has seen me cry.

At dinner, Grandma stood abruptly from the table, her food untouched. She stalked up to her room and slammed the door. Noah and I glanced at each other but resumed conversation for Zoe's sake.

A few minutes later, Grandma came down the steps, a piece of paper held aloft. "I see what's going on here. I see what you people are doing!"

"Mom, what are you talking about?"

"The sour cream." A beady squint. "You gave it to Zoe. But it is mine! I have the receipt!"

I looked at the paper she was waving. "Mom, that receipt's from June. It's November now. You didn't buy this sour cream. Do you really think you're being taken advantage of here?"

"Yes! That is exactly what I think! You did not give me the sour cream. You gave me cheap yogurt!"

"Your plate is identical to Zoe's. Would you like to try hers to see? I can get you a spoon. And even if you *had* bought the sour cream, would you be so against sharing it with your granddaughter?"

This quieted her, but I didn't stop. Something in me came loose.

"You're living with us for free, Mom. I cook your meals. I launder your clothes. When you go to the bathroom after you digest this dinner, the paper you wipe yourself with? I bought that, too. Yet you come downstairs and tell me *I'm* taking advantage of *you*?"

"Well, I guess I'm not very nice. That's your point, eh? Put me in a nursing home, then. I should not be around you when I am like this."

"Mom—"

"No, no. You are right. My head does not work anymore."

"It's okay. You should sit. Please, Mom, let's just eat."

She looked at me sadly, a terrible, defeated look. She shook her head and went back upstairs.

When her door softly closed, I burst into tears. Zoe stared and then giggled, embarrassed. She turned to Noah, alarmed.

"Mommy," Zoe said urgently, climbing out of her chair. "Mommy, don't cry." She flung her little arms around my neck.

As I tuck her in, her question about Grandma is earnest.

"Sometimes Grandma doesn't know what she's saying," I explain. "She doesn't mean her words. We have to be patient. It isn't always easy. Tonight . . . she hurt my feelings, but she didn't mean to."

"Is that why you cried?"

"Yes. Grown-ups cry sometimes, and that's okay."

It is such an obvious statement, straight out of a sitcom, but I can tell I've just exploded her world. You know sometimes as a parent when your child has folded something into her memory. This, The Thing With The Sour Cream, will one day come up in conversation, maybe in a college class ("When did you first see your parents as people?") or with a partner ("Your grandmother lived with you when you were a kid?").

From that day forward, Zoe acts differently toward Grandma. She no longer sees her as a co-conspirator. She recognizes that Grandma needs help.

She takes her hand when we're somewhere unfamiliar. She helps buckle her seatbelt because Grandma's hand tremor makes fastening it difficult. While she once would have giggled if Grandma unloaded the dirty dishes or hid her purse, she no longer laughs.

The shift in Zoe isn't caused by Grandma having acted worse. The Thing With The Sour Cream is a big deal because Zoe saw me cry.

I realize that if I constantly play the superhero as a mom, my daughter will never know my struggles. If my only reaction to Grandma's odd behavior is to resume conversation as though nothing happened, I am doing my daughter a disservice.

*Too much strength can be a weakness, you know.*

My tears showed Zoe that Grandma's behavior isn't isolated or silly, that it affects me deeply, that we are interconnected. She learns that she can help Grandma—and help me. She learns that she has an important part to play.

If for no other reason, our time with Grandma is worth it for this, for the growth of my daughter's already great big heart.

# 41

If a story attempts to assert a truth, the listener's assumptions can derail that story. They can cause it to not be heard.

Whenever I tell people that my family is Indian, I get the impression that they don't hear what comes next. It's like they have cotton in their ears. It doesn't matter if I speak of a lovely flat with servants or of an imperious Brahmin mother. They nod and smile, but hear *poverty, third world, came here for a better life.*

When you encounter assumptions often enough, you start to harbor them. You do this without even realizing it.

I thought that my mother's financial fretting was a function of her immigrant status. Any piece of mail caused a cascade of worries. My brother and I joked about it. "She's been here for forty years, but she still acts like she could get arrested at the DMV," we said.

This could be why it takes me so long to see it. Her preoccupation with money has nothing to do with being an immigrant. It's anxiety, pure and simple. I'm the daughter of a psychiatrist, after all. I should have thought to mention her symptoms to doctors, should have seen the behaviors right before my eyes. Instead there was cotton in my ears. All I heard was *immigrant immigrant immigrant.*

The constant rustling of financial documents, the obsessive

quality to the notes she scrawls, the fact that she can't go ten minutes without asking if her house has sold: These are the overtime workings of an anxious mind.

When Zoe tries to talk to her, she no longer listens. When we go for walks, she doesn't notice the birds or the trees. She doesn't smile, even if it's a glorious day. The wheels keep turning in her mind. No wonder she's exhausted. She interrupts Zoe in the middle of a "knock, knock" joke to ask me about her taxes. Her baseline assumption is panic. It puts cotton in her ears, too.

# 42

In January, I take my mom to see Dr. Singh again. She suggests antianxiety medication.

My mom shakes her head. "The side effects exacerbate dementia."

"That's a minor effect you're talking about. It's negligible, especially when—"

"Negligible!" my mom interrupts. *"Negligible?"*

"You don't seem to be enjoying day-to-day life," Dr. Singh points out.

"What's to enjoy? I have been anxious my whole life. I am used to it."

"Mom, that makes no sense." Diplomacy has never been my strong suit. "Even if the drugs speed up your condition, who cares? Aren't four good years better than five bad ones?"

She glares at me as though her happiness isn't my business. It is, though, when she lives in my house.

"She'll never take that medication voluntarily," I tell Dr. Singh after my mom leaves the room. "She's too stubborn. But her mood . . . I don't know how much more I can take."

"You mentioned anxiety, but it sounds like there are also signs of depression?"

"She's been muttering under her breath that she wants to die. Maybe because it's winter and dark out—I'm sure that isn't helping—but she doesn't want to come on walks. She's retreating. She wants to sleep all day."

Dr. Singh makes notes.

"The thing is, I have a young daughter. I worry about what she's getting exposed to. It was one thing when my mom had tantrums. I could explain those. But this sort of daily negativity . . . it's hard. On everyone."

Dr. Singh nods thoughtfully. "She's done so well with you, you know. Her physical improvement is remarkable. If we can find a way to keep her with you, that would be ideal."

I look away. "Family is best" is what caretakers often get told, I think to encourage us, but it's a sentiment that hits me hard. It adds to the pressure. I decide to voice what's on my mind, a question that made Noah and my brother uncomfortable when I raised the possibility with them.

"What if we give her something without telling her what it is? I mean, I don't even know if that's allowed, ethically speaking. . . ."

"You're her caretaker. Do you think it would work?"

"She'll take whatever I give her. I just need a way of explaining a new pill. It can't have anything to do with mood or the brain."

"Hmm. If it were up to you, what would you say?"

I can't believe Dr. Singh is playing along, that she isn't reprimanding me. "I guess I'd say it was for her bones. She's always going on about osteoporosis."

"So you'd say it's a supplement? To improve bone health?"

"Yes." I nod, relieved. "That's exactly the sort of thing she'd go for."

Dr. Singh pages the nurse to have my mom brought back into the room. Smoothly, she explains she wants to put her on a supplement to increase bone density.

My mother nods. "Osteoporosis, yes, this is a concern for someone my age. . . ."

Bone health. This is the story we tell her to get her on board.

I don't know what the medical guidelines are when treating cognitive impairment. I don't know how different physicians handle these dilemmas. I know that in a novel, the scene with Dr. Singh wouldn't fly. "A doctor can't lie to a patient," I imagine the reader saying.

Noah can't believe it, either. "A bone supplement," he repeats. "Seriously?"

All I know is that after about two weeks, my mom's mood lightens. She stops rustling through her financial papers. She stops asking if her house has sold. She stops saying that she wants to die.

She once knew more about medication than anyone. It's inconceivable to me that she takes an unnamed pill. Yet every night I open an orange bottle whose prescription sticker I've removed. "Your supplement," I say, solicitous as a butler.

She doesn't ask questions. If she did, I don't know how I'd respond.

Maybe it speaks to her trust in me, or maybe it reflects her decline. Sometimes, though, I wonder if she knows she's being duped. Maybe she prefers the story to the truth.

She must sense changes in herself. Even if she can't perceive her altered mood, she must notice her increased appetite and deeper sleep. I suspect Dr. Singh took these side effects into account when selecting the drug. Fifteen milligrams of mirtazapine. I imagine it's the sort of brilliant clinical choice my mom once made.

A hungry patient is easier to feed. Meals become less of a hassle. Having her go to bed early makes life easier for me and Noah. I can go to the gym without worrying that she'll throw a fit in my absence.

Really, though, it's the change in her disposition that's astounding. She notices the birds when we go on walks. She smiles at strangers and says hello.

"Mom's cheerful," I tell my brother. "She's *pleasant*."

"Huh," he says.

I wonder what her life would have been like if she'd started the medication sooner. Maybe she would have gone on vacation. Maybe she would have bought a house she liked. Maybe she wouldn't have quit her job. She might have stopped to feel the sun on her face instead of worrying about the rain. I suppose it's natural when someone changes for the better: You wish you could have helped them sooner.

# 43

As my mom's mood continues to brighten, I turn increasingly grumpy.

I should be happy. She's doing so well. When she was thorny and awful, I was sympathetic. Now that she's thriving, I feel hostile—maybe because for the first time, I see what her presence costs us.

Our world has shrunk. I didn't see it before, in the adrenaline-fueled rush of those first few months. Now that she's easier, I can view our situation clearly.

We have adjusted to make her life better. We orbit around her, tiptoeing around our own house. After dinner, Noah and I talk in whispers. We sneak down to the basement if we want to watch a movie, because otherwise she plops down on the couch between us. Zoe's snacks go up on a high shelf because otherwise Grandma gobbles them up. We tape signs to the stove so she won't turn it on and walk away.

I am tired of finding my underwear in her room, of wiping that green medicinal solution from the floor, of our agonizingly slow walks. I'm tired of being unable to leave the house during the day because I can't leave her alone. Really, I am just tired.

I miss spending time with Zoe and Noah, just the three of us. I miss focusing on my daughter.

I've been stalled on my novel. I haven't bothered applying for various teaching opportunities or writing residencies. What's the point, if I can't be away?

I can't remember the last time we invited friends over. I don't know when it happened exactly, when we stopped socializing, but it dawns on me that it's been months. I don't know if friends stopped inviting us out or if we've self-isolated. I feel like we're on the other side of a wall.

My mom takes up the whole house. Even when she's in her room with the door closed, I feel aware of her. She dictates our rhythms and moods. Her slippered footfalls govern my days.

As she grows, we diminish. Life narrows to vegetarian meals and board games and the sound of her sniffs and snorts. She no longer brings up assisted living facilities. Why should she? My house has become one.

Physically, she has swelled, requiring new clothes every few months. It reminds me of when Zoe was a baby. The size-zero pants in the closet have been joined by stacks of twos and fours. Now her sixes are snug.

Meanwhile, I've lost weight. My workouts have intensified in relation to my stress. At dinner I peck at my food, wanting only a glass of wine. I go down in size while she goes up. Soon she's wearing my old clothes while I wear her discards.

"Are those your mom's pants?" Noah asks one day, frowning.

"Oh," I say defensively, "I mean, she hardly ever wore them. And it's not like I have time to shop."

We are trading places. She's the one saying to me, "Should we go for a walk? It's so nice out!" while I mutter beneath my breath and shuffle reluctantly out the door.

# 44

Who is it I am caring for? Sometimes I wonder who inhabits the guest room. I'm not so sure it's my mom.

She is a ghost, with her shuffling footsteps and shock of white hair. She goes for days without speaking. She wanders in and out of rooms, sits with us at dinner. At night I wake to the creaking of her door.

They say that animals perceive information that humans can't. Lola has a trick she loves performing for beloved family members. She brings a sock, matching it to the right person, then sits on the person's foot, sock held high, tail thwacking the floor loudly, as if to say, *Look! I know you and love you and claim you.*

Whenever Lola saw my mom in the past, she would do this. Since Grandma moved in with us, Lola hasn't done it once. If I prompt her ("Where's Grandma's sock?"), Lola looks away, embarrassed for me. She is perfectly nice to Grandma. She just won't claim her. It's as if she already knows what it has taken so long for me to see. The person living with us isn't really my mother anymore.

Looking at my mom, I'm reminded of someone on life support whose vital signs are at the bare minimum. She eats what I give her to eat. She wears what I tell her to wear. She trails me, cheerful but vacant. The monitors beep and hum and tell me she's alive, but from her passive expression I glean nothing.

# 45

Noah works from home one day so that I can go into the city. I need—and this is clear to everyone—a break.

Caregiver burnout. I stumble upon the term online. Feeling tired and run-down. Overreacting to minor nuisances. Trouble concentrating. Difficulty relaxing. Loss of appetite. Insomnia. Check, check, check.

I wander the city aimlessly, block after block, and though it is a drizzly day, I savor the experience. I walk from Grand Central to SoHo, zigzagging the blocks. On my way back uptown, I pause in front of the Union Square Café, glimpsing the welcoming interior.

I duck inside and take a seat at the bar. For the first time in weeks, I am hungry. I order a bowl of soup, the perfect antidote to the rain and chill. The space is calm and unpretentious. A long mahogany bar gleams beneath the mirrors and lights. A console table holds yellow ranunculus and forsythia and Meyer lemons: signs that spring has sprung. My soup arrives, steaming in its bowl, accompanied by a thick slice of bread, gloriously amber in color, with a sunshiny swirl of butter.

That lunch restores me. Every object—white cloth napkins, water glasses pleasant to hold, fragrant rosemary in the soup— works on my senses. The hum of conversation, the gentle clang of cutlery, the coming and going of patrons: All of it reminds me of the world beyond my mother, a world of civility.

Heading home, I try to hold on to my restored goodwill, but I feel it start to drain. I sense my mom waiting for me. There is the dinner I need to cook, the sheets I need to launder. When I enter her room, I know I will find chocolate beneath the pillows, socks in the vase, her purse in its strange new hiding spot.

How long will I do this? It was the question everyone once asked. Months later, I feel myself contemplating it in earnest.

I always imagined reaching a point where I could no longer care for her. I envisioned a dramatic episode, some incontrovertible turning point (a violent confrontation; the loss of bladder control) that made her need for help obvious. I imagined Noah and I shaking our heads ruefully and telling people we had no choice.

Never did I imagine the change would come from me.

I don't know it until that lunch. A simple meal shouldn't feel that good. It's like finally turning on a light and then, once your eyes have adjusted, realizing you've been in the dark.

Before getting on the train, I buy a bundle of forsythia from a stall at Grand Central—a last attempt to hold on to my afternoon away. Yellow flowers on brown branches get wrapped in white paper. As the train whisks me back, I see to my chagrin bushes of forsythia growing along the tracks. I laugh when I get home. We have clusters of it in the backyard. How ridiculous to pay for something growing wild—though maybe if I hadn't bought it, I wouldn't have noticed. Maybe we pay to be reminded of beauty, to see what was always already before our eyes. I see what I've been missing, which has nothing to do with lunch or flowers and everything to do with growing free.

# 46

That makes complete sense," my brother says when I tell him about caregiver burnout. I had hoped my feelings would pass, that they were just a phase. I thought that if I did something nice for myself like treat myself to lunch, those feelings would go away. Weeks later, nothing has changed. I'm fried.

My mom didn't want to burden her children. She was explicit about this. It was why she signed up for long-term care all those years ago.

I know this is what she wanted, but I don't know how to do it. I wish I could have my old mom back for a day. I want my former mom to help me with my current one.

"So what do you want to do?" my brother asks.

I'm glad he makes me say the words. I need to be the one to say them.

"I think it's time. I think we should look into care facilities. I think . . ." I swallow. "I think I'm done."

# III

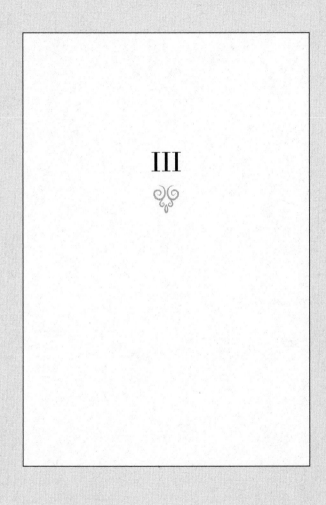

# 1

If I have fashioned myself into a crutch for my mother, the reverse is also true. She has become my crutch. I take validation in caring for her. I've stopped seeing my self-worth outside of my role as a caretaker.

Soon after my mom came to live with us, I told Noah that we should have another child. "Think about it. Zoe's seven. Soon she'll be a teen! And Lola . . . she doesn't have much time left. One day Grandma will be gone. The house will be empty!" Panic filled my voice. "I'm thirty-seven! We should have another while we still can!"

Adding to our family seemed like a natural extension of what I was learning: To be needed is a gift, life is beautiful in its chaotic complexity, and we can handle more than we think.

We tried to get pregnant. Only when the tests came back negative, when stick after stick failed to show a plus sign, did I realize I wasn't disappointed. I was relieved. I had talked myself into the idea of another child, but in hindsight, I was motivated more by fear than desire.

To be needed is a gift, yes, but it can also be a way of hiding. A child should never be compensatory, there "just in case." Those words represented my mom's philosophy. I'm not sure I want them to be mine.

I think of her other guiding words: *hang in there.* "You just need to hang in there a little longer," she'd tell me, or, "I just need to hang in there with this job." She probably said it to herself quite a bit when she was married to my dad.

I don't want to hang in there. I want to thrive. I want this for my sake, but also for Zoe's. I want to show her that women *can* thrive, that we don't have to be overburdened, that our value isn't in our sacrifice. I want to show her that we are our own best thing.

Surely there are ways of being needed that don't involve raising offspring or caring for the elderly. Writing a book, for example. Isn't this, too, a way of giving? On the lovely occasion that I receive a note from a reader, it always opens the same way: by thanking me.

Nervously, I start looking into assisted living facilities. The costs are staggering. Reputable places run between seven and ten thousand dollars a month.

I call her insurance company. "She's fully covered," the person reports.

"For ten thousand a month?" I ask in disbelief.

"Yup."

"For how long?"

"Indefinitely."

I think about how she signed up for coverage when she was still sharp. I think about her modest house, her modest clothes. *I never want to burden my children,* she said. I once found the statement burdensome. Now I rethink her words. She had planned. How she had planned! She had anticipated this very moment.

Women are said to be natural caretakers. I've always resented the implications. I want to believe that daughters aren't hardwired to give up our needs.

One day, perhaps there will exist a country where men serve

as caretakers in equal proportion to women. I picture this imaginary place, filled with women engineers and stay-at-home dads, multigenerational households of new configurations, the tired old gender roles out the window.

I want that future, but for now there is reality. Women in the United States provide the bulk of caregiving for parents and in-laws. I think about these women, women whose parents weren't obsessed with long-term life insurance the way my mom was. I think about women spread too thin between work and marriage and motherhood, women who have no choice but to "hang in there" because no one in their lives worried about the "just in case."

When I tore my calf muscle, Noah unearthed a pair of crutches from our garage. I hadn't thought to question their provenance, but their origin finally dawns on me. I nearly laugh out loud. They're the Frost Valley crutches. My mom had saved them for two decades.

I picture her on her last day at the Long Island house, about to set off for her new life in New Jersey. She could have taken photo albums, wedding gifts, expensive saris, beloved mementos. Instead she took a pair of crutches. *Just in case,* I can hear her thinking.

She didn't always know how to care for me the way I wanted. She cared for me the way she knew how. Seeing how she planned for me and my brother, I see that she loved us—of course she loved us—maybe not in ways that spoke to me, but in ways that made sense to her.

I don't have an imprint of my palm from kindergarten. I don't have framed pictures of the two of us. I have no letters from her. I have aluminum crutches and an ironclad insurance policy. That was my mother.

She wouldn't have wanted me living this way, sprinting in

and out of my office to mop up her spilled dental solution or prepare her a meal. She would have been horrified. The part of her that held strong opinions is the part I miss most.

As a young girl, I perceived her as preoccupied. I thought her career was the reason, but that isn't quite right. She was drained by her marriage, by the constant, exhausting question of whether to leave. She wanted to, but didn't know how to go about it. What ultimately exhausts the woman in the river is her fear and her guilt.

I am in danger of replicating my mother's state. I am in an untenable situation that takes away from my ability to be there for my daughter. Zoe doesn't share stories of gym class and recess with me. She can tell that I'm weighed down.

*Let go.* I feel the words coming from my old mom, the one who knew what it meant to stand in the river. She wouldn't have said it gently or lovingly. She would have barked it. *Are you crazy? What are you doing? You are going to drown!*

Her insurance policy is a life raft. It isn't accompanied by heartfelt words. She never said to me, "I love you and want you to feel me thinking of you even when I'm gone." Her planning is a missive from her former self, filled with words she could never say. *Live your life. Be happy. Let me go.*

# 2

Guilt and worry. I whip back and forth between them. The thought of moving her out, the knowledge of how hard the transition will be for her, is overwhelming.

I ask my brother to call Dr. Singh and Kathy to share our decision. I can't be the one to do it. I feel too guilty. "They'll arrange to send her medical files to the insurance company," my brother reports back. "Did they object?" I ask. "Were they surprised?" "No," my brother says, confused. "They were the ones who recommended assisted living in the first place, remember?"

Oh. Right. I think back to when I first brought her home to live with me. *I can't imagine putting her in a home right now,* I had told my brother. I didn't think she was ready. She was, though. She had been for some time. My brother had known it. I was the one who wasn't ready to let her go.

A neighbor tells me about an assisted living facility ten minutes away. Her father lives there. She says it's a wonderful place with caring staff. I arrange for a tour.

I'm prepared for surly nurses and dimly lit rooms, the pervasive smell of disinfectant, catatonic patients getting rolled by in wheelchairs. When I walk in, I hear singing.

"Don't mind us," the director says with a smile. "It's happy hour."

I'm standing in a double height lobby with a stone fireplace that could be the entry of a boutique hotel. To the right is a bar. Residents are gathered around a microphone, belting out Sinatra tunes in front of a karaoke machine. People sip wine and nibble on snacks.

The director leads me to the dining hall, where flowers sit on each table. I meet the chef, an Egyptian man thrilled by the prospect of an Indian resident. "Finally! I'll get to use some spices!" he says, beaming.

In the upstairs café area, residents read the newspaper. Others work on a puzzle with mugs of tea. There's a library, a garden, a movie room, a gym. I find a list of daily activities, which includes everything from yoga to a stock market club.

Usually, the director tells me, it's the prospective resident—they prefer not to say "patient"—who arranges for a tour. A person in the early stages of Alzheimer's recognizes the need for help. The thought of assistance brings relief. It's the family members who object.

I think back to when my mom quit her job. *I am old now,* she said. *I can no longer be who I was.* She spoke the words. I refused to listen.

"How do I get her to consider coming here?" I ask the director. "She's so comfortable at my house."

"With someone as far along as your mom, we recommend a pretext. You might say you're renovating your home, for example. Or you might tell her you're going away on a long trip."

"Oh."

"It helps with the transition. Soon, of course, the person forgets whatever reason brought them in. It usually takes a month or two, but they adjust."

I reflect back on when my mom moved in, how I told her she just needed to bring her weight up and then she could go back to her house. That was a pretext, too. The difference was that I believed it.

# 3

I find it difficult to talk about my mom with others. Even at the linguistic level, I don't know what words to use. Was/is. Past/present. "My mom was a psychiatrist," I might say. "No, no, she's still alive," I quickly add, seeing the person's expression.

Even that statement, "She's still alive," feels misleading. The phrase "quality of life" exists in healthcare for this reason, to assess whether daily life is meaningful. This is difficult to gauge with Alzheimer's because the organ making that determination is precisely what's affected.

If my mom spends twenty hours in bed, how alive is she? If she doesn't remember how she spent the morning, doesn't remember what I gave her for lunch, doesn't remember our conversation from five minutes ago, what state is she in? What is the present without the past? What kind of verb is that?

Before she started taking her antianxiety medication, she would mutter that she didn't want to live this way. Was it depression or lucidity? She recognized her lack of verb tense. Who could blame her for rejecting it?

It's all so thorny that even the medical community shies away from the issue. States like Washington and California that have "die with dignity" laws don't permit end-of-life measures for Alzheimer's patients. We don't want someone making major decisions in a compromised state. This makes sense. On the other hand, Alzheimer's is terminal. Anyone diagnosed with it knows what awaits: a slow decline leading to the loss of bowel and bladder control, gross motor control, and, eventually, the ability to swallow food. Diapers and a feeding tube await my mother, a state difficult to place on the ontological spectrum. It's no way to be.

I'm reminded of the verb tenses I learned while studying French: past perfect, conditional. Maybe that describes it. The past was perfect. Everything now feels conditional.

I want to assemble a new verb tense for Alzheimer's: conditional past perfect. Sometimes, under the right conditions, my old mom shows herself. I get a tantalizing few minutes with Former Mom. Our reunion is too brief. I feel my memory glorifying her, preserving her, making its tactful erasures.

The past perfect in French is actually called the *plus-que-parfait,* which means "more than perfect." That might be the truest description of all. The buried past is beyond perfect. It gets to stay that way.

Is/was. Here/gone. Sometimes when I look at her I feel she's not really there. Sometimes I think she left long ago. That might be the better question: Where are you, Mom?

Perhaps she is back in India, an indulged girl in Bombay, watching her lovebirds and squirrels, Ruby following her from room to room, servants in the background, her father holding out a gift. Maybe that's where she is, in the buried past, the more-than-perfect. I am on the outside, tapping at the glass.

# 4

How do you get rid of a ghost?

The mom who purchased long-term care insurance isn't the mom who lives with me. "Oh!" she says contentedly whenever we return from one of our walks. "It's so nice to be home!"

*Home is the place that's always open,* Zoe once said, the place that doesn't turn you away—yet I am about to do just that to my own mother.

Her cheerfulness has multiplied. Her attachment to me has bloomed. "What should we do this weekend? What are we having for dinner?" It is a reliance I encouraged. These are crutches I fashioned.

Outside, the spring flowers have opened, a profusion of vivid hues. On our afternoon walks, she likes to point out color. "See that red!" she exclaims in Marathi. "How vibrant it is!" She is filled with wonder, marveling over yellows and pinks. It is a dotty innocence from which I recoil.

I want her to be more than this. I want her to be the teller of stories, the healer of patients who gets accosted in public, such is her legendary brilliance. I want her to be a fierce matriarch, batting away the crutches I offer.

I don't want to make up a story about the assisted living facility. I don't want to invent a pretext about renovations or travel. I want us to have an earnest talk as mother and daughter. She deserves that much.

Living with her has meant reexamining who I thought she was: the mom in my mind versus my mom as she existed. She used to be mythic. She became real. I decide to talk with her openly.

Noah and I sit her down one afternoon. "So, Mom," I say, "we wanted to talk with you. As you've always said, we can't keep you here forever."

"Right." Her eyes do a panicky dart around the room.

"A neighbor," I say hurriedly, "mentioned an assisted living facility just a few minutes away. It received excellent reviews. I figured we could check it out."

"Oh." She nods. I sound, I imagine, eminently reasonable. "Do they take my insurance?" she finally asks.

"Yes."

"Do they have vegetarian food?"

"They do. They'll even make you Indian food."

"Hmm."

"They have a garden, a library, a gym. It seems nice."

"Well, I'm glad you found this place."

"You are?"

"Absolutely. That way if anything happens to me, we will have a plan. It's good to think ahead. Just in case."

I start to say something but stop. Noah looks at me, horrified.

"It's true," she continues. "Right now I am independent, but say that were to change. For example, if I were to break my hip. Osteoporosis is a concern, you know."

I clear my throat. "This place . . . it has a special memory care unit."

She blinks. "Geriatric fractures! They are very common."

I save my exasperation until Noah and I can talk privately that night. "Fractures!" I explode. "Osteoporosis!"

He shakes his head. "Honey, what are we going to do?"

The next day, she calls up relatives. "Maya is shipping me off to a nursing home in upstate New York!" she tells them. "It will be four or five hours away, in the middle of nowhere. Like Siberia! I will not have access to phone or email. Who knows what will happen to me? I will spend three hours every day in a swimming pool. They make you go in cold water!"

I only know about these calls because relatives contact me, alarmed. I assure them that I'm not sending my mom upstate to swimming camp.

I want to record these conversations and play them back for her. I want to show her the underwear in the vase and the chocolate under the pillow. If only I could persuade her with evidence and reasoning, then she would see my side of the story—and isn't understanding a hair away from forgiveness?

That's when it hits me. My desire to have an earnest talk with her isn't for her sake. It's for mine.

She is no longer capable of an earnest talk. She needs a story. I have to be the one to provide it, to sugarcoat this pill. The thought of the pretext is painful because it means accepting her decline. The pretext means saying farewell to my old mom. Telling her a story means accepting the truth.

# 5

Life might be a series of competing narratives, of casting out and attempting to reel in the right words. *This is who I am. This is what I do.* As we reach for new words, we try to find ourselves in them.

A family is a battleground of such stories. When I look back on my childhood, I see everyone's competing tales. We fought for control: my dad, my mom, my brother, me. We wanted to establish ourselves.

Every family knows this tension. "He's the athletic one." "She's the artsy one." Ask anyone about her family and some version of the above comes out. "My parents wanted me to be more like my brother," or, "My sister was the black sheep." If family members were asked, they would object, offering their own versions of what transpired.

This is why the holidays can be stressful. Stories collide at the table. In your own life, you can establish your own narrative. You don't have to be the athletic one or the artsy one. You can exist on your own terms.

Freedom, on some level, is the right to tell one's story. We tell stories to assert ourselves, as a constantly morphing declaration of self. "We tell stories," as Joan Didion put it, "in order to live." The telling of stories isn't a pastime. It isn't a way to distract us from life. It is life.

Perhaps my mother's greatest gift to me was that she let my stories exist, gave them room to breathe. She didn't censor or edit me.

What I recognize now—what I could not admit before—is that this wasn't a conscious choice on her part. It wasn't a strategy. She didn't reject helicopter parenting because she knew better. She was tired, exhausted, overworked, overwhelmed. I chose to think otherwise. I didn't want to see myself as the object of neglect. I wanted to believe I was the careful result of excellent choices. I wanted to believe she was holding me, even as I treaded water.

Her gifts to me may have been inadvertent, but that doesn't mean they weren't gifts. There is beauty in listening to a story in progress, in trusting the storyteller to find her own way.

My father wasn't capable of this. He couldn't bear to see me strike out into the world on my terms. He saw me as a reflection of him. He wanted to control that reflection. My mom didn't take my explorations of self personally, perhaps for the simple reason that she was distracted.

What I learned from being her daughter and then her caretaker is that the audience plays a crucial role. As a parent, so often I fool myself into thinking I should be speaking (lecturing, explaining, counseling) when, really, I should sit back and not say a word. To love this way means ceding the reins. It is excruciating.

There is an easy kind of love I give Zoe, one that comes readily, without cost or much effort. I can hug, soothe, console, reassure. To praise a crayon drawing or wipe her tears when she scrapes a knee—it is not difficult. Then there is a harder love, a love I have to reach for when feeling cornered. When we are in public and Zoe throws a tantrum, when we visit friends and she doesn't behave according to plan, I feel a shadow of what my father must have felt. I have to remind myself not to take such moments personally, that they are part of childhood and growth. My daughter cannot settle into better versions of herself unless she tries them out. While it is my job to help her see the effects of her choices, it is not my job to prevent her from making them. I have to let her find her own way.

What happens to the woman after she emerges from the river? Whatever her choice, she will have to explain herself. This, her story, might define her more than her choice, not just because it is the face she presents to the world but because it is the face she presents to herself. Her story is what she lives with.

"I decided it was time. I moved my mother into a facility." One day I will need to speak these words—to relatives, to friends. I can barely speak them to myself.

"I sent my child away for three years." My mom never said it, but it was what she did. "I didn't have the courage to leave my husband, so I watched my daughter leave instead." She did that, too. She created a story for herself that made her choices palatable: "Everything I did was for my children."

I wonder now what she told my brother. When she packed up his clothes and toys, she must have murmured to him— what? "It is only for a short time." "I will be with you soon." He was only two years old, but she must have felt compelled to say something, if only to soothe herself. It was a pretext to help them both. It was a story she told so that she could live.

# 6

It is May now. She once worried about assisted living facilities while I told her to relax. Now I'm the one agonizing over them while she floats along, serene.

I research different options—Indian facilities, places in New Jersey and Connecticut, centers that specialize in dementia. The one I visited strikes me as the best bet. Residents looked happy, and I like that it's close by.

Still, I can't imagine her there. As nice as it was, she will be miserable. She isn't like those Sinatra-belting seniors. She's introverted and judgmental. I picture her holed up in her room, refusing to go for a walk or explore the garden. I picture her lecturing the doctors, pointing out their diagnostic errors.

"Maybe we should keep her with us," Noah takes to saying. "It might be easier."

The first time he says it, I feel terribly guilty. He's right. We *should* keep her.

Over time, though, it occurs to me that he isn't the one caring for her all day. His fear of the transition blinds him to my needs. It hurts. At times I want to wave my hands in front of his face. *Don't you see me?* I want to shout. *Don't you see me here, exhausted?*

Where is the husband in the story of the woman in the river? Where are the relatives and neighbors, the nosy aunties and meddlesome in-laws? Even in India, even in multigenerational households, even when women are supposed to have support, we stand in the river alone. Too often, decisions fall on our shoulders. Even if we have caring spouses and helpful siblings, such moments feel solitary.

The story of the woman in the river ends with her standing in the current, paralyzed. It is how I feel, unable to make a decision while the water around me rises. I've been telling myself that I don't know what to say to my mother, but that isn't true at all. The truth is that I don't know how to live with myself, how to do what I know I must.

# 7

---

M om, you once told me a story," I say on a walk one day. "You said your mom told it to you. It was a myth about a woman in a river, holding a child in her arms—"

"Oh!" She stops abruptly and turns to me. "You remember that? You have such a good memory. I have not thought of that story in years!"

"I tried to look it up. I didn't know if it was a myth or if it was based on a Hindu parable of some kind. I can't find anything on it."

"Hmm."

"Is there any chance *Agi* invented it?"

"She was not a writer, if that's what you mean. You are the only storyteller in the family." She chuckles.

"What really gets me is the ending. Or lack of ending, I should say."

"What do you mean?"

"Well, we don't know what the woman in the river chooses."

"Of course we do. She lets go of her child."

She says this so matter-of-factly I think I've imagined it. "What?" I laugh. "Mom, that's not what happens. The woman stands there. You said . . . you said we can't know what she chooses until we are in the river ourselves."

"Is that what I said?" She looks bemused. "No, the way my

mother told it is that the woman lets go." Seeing my shocked expression, her features soften. "I must have changed it to protect you. Perhaps it seemed too harsh."

"So . . . the story just ends like that? With her letting go of her baby?"

She shrugs. "Indian stories, you know. They can be quite strange."

We walk for a few minutes, my mom sniffling and snorting and humming in her off-key way. My question feels even more pressing now.

"The thing is, how does the woman live with herself?"

"What woman?" My mom has forgotten our conversation. I take her through it again, this time not sharing how she revised the story.

"Yes, yes," she says. "The woman in the river. What is your question?"

"Well, I mean, how does she do it? How does she let go?"

"She just does."

"Come on, Mom, it can't be that simple. She must regret it, right? Does she reach for her child, realizing her mistake? Does she spend the rest of her life filled with regret?"

"No."

"But Mom—"

"She has let go. That is the point."

"That doesn't answer the question of *how*."

"You are asking the wrong question."

"I am?" I don't even know what I'm asking anymore.

"You imagine the woman still holding on to the child after she has let go. That is your error. The story is not about her letting go."

"It isn't?"

"The story is about the woman choosing herself. Once she makes that choice, everything follows."

Oh. The way she puts it makes the story a positive one, not a story of loss and anguish, but one of hope. A story with a future tense. It occurs to me how right my mother is.

When I glance up, I see that she is several feet ahead. I hurry to catch up. "Do you think it's possible? For a woman to choose herself? Do you think . . . do you think she ends up happy?"

"Of course. Why wouldn't she?"

"But what about the child who drowns?"

"Who said anything about him drowning?"

"You're saying he *lives*?"

"You never know in Indian myths. Perhaps a bird comes and lifts him away."

Her mouth twitches. We laugh. Soon we are laughing harder than we should, harder than the situation warrants. "Can you imagine? The baby held in the bird's beak?" It sets us off, howling, maybe because it's so exactly in keeping with Indian myths, or maybe because it feels so good to laugh that we don't want to stop.

"And then the deer in the forest would feed him!"

"And provide him shelter!"

"And he would grow up to be king!"

"Of course!"

We laugh so hard we wipe our tears.

The woman chooses herself.

Once she makes that choice, everything follows.

Could it really be that simple?

# 8

I will camp in the backyard."

"I will sleep on the kitchen floor."

"Why can't I stay with your brother?"

These are her replies when I tell her we are renovating the house.

At night, she slips letters under my bedroom door, heartbreaking letters begging me to let her stay. She promises to be good. She threatens to sue me. She laments having such selfish children. I wake up to three, four, five a morning.

"It's just for a few weeks, Mom."

"Why can't I stay with you?"

I don't engage with her suggestions. I hold firm and repeat the same line. *It's just for a few weeks.* I speak to her as though speaking to a child.

Meanwhile I order items I know she will need: a shower curtain, a bath mat, a trash can. An electric kettle in case she ever wants to make tea. It's like sending my kid off to college.

I live with a wall in my life—on one side, her protests, on the other, my preparations. The two sides contradict each other. I assure her and soothe her ("It's just for a few weeks, Mom") while I set up her new phone and cable service with annual contracts. I have no idea how these two sides will reconcile. The wall makes the situation bearable, but the wall is untenable.

"So this is only for a few weeks?" she says as she watches me pack her suitcase.

"Yup."

"And then I will move back in with you?"

"Absolutely."

She pauses. "What if you like life without me? What if you get used to having things be easier? You will not want me back."

I hug her. "I'll always want you around, Mom." This much I know to be true.

She relaxes against me. "Okay," she says into my shoulder. "I will make the best of it, knowing it is only for a little while."

The next morning I wake up to find a half dozen letters under my door. The letters are a bouquet of personalities, some pleading, some perplexing, some poisonous. When I come downstairs, she tells me she has the answer. She will sleep outside in a tent. So it continues, right until move-in day.

·

# 9

On a bright day in June, the sky a cloudless blue, almost exactly a year after she moved in with me, I move my mom into the assisted living facility. Right away, it is a nightmare.

"When do I need to be at breakfast? How will I know when meals are?"

"You can eat anytime, Mom. You just go to the dining hall."

"Where is that? How do I get there?"

"I put up signs for you. See?" Around her room I've taped up signs in thirty-six-point font. *You can eat whenever you want. Go straight down the hall for meals. If you have any questions, push the button on your necklace.*

I chose this particular room for my mom because it is one of three units on the ground floor, a straight shot to the dining hall. Unlike other residents, she won't have to take an elevator or negotiate the confusing upstairs corridors, which all look alike.

"What if I don't remember to look at the signs? What if they don't have vegetarian food? What if they try to make me do things? I am not social. Oh, this is all too much!" Her body is rigid with fear. She trembles from head to toe.

"Listen, Mom, I'm staying with you for lunch. I'm coming back with Noah and Zoe for dinner. You're not alone."

Earlier in the day, I dropped off her favorite Indian meal at the dining hall. I figured it would help address her fears about the food and make a good impression.

"How is it?" I ask after she takes a bite.

She dips her head. "Not as good as at your house," she mutters.

I want to smack my forehead. I can't tell her that it's the exact same dish.

At the end of the meal, she grabs my arm. "Why do you have to go? What if they abuse me here?"

"Mom, I'm coming back in three hours."

At dinner that evening, Zoe scans the menu. "They have mac and cheese! And veggie burgers! And ice cream! Grandma, this place is fantastic!"

My mom does not smile.

We lead her back to her room after dinner. We're there when the med tech comes in. "Your supplement," he says. He smiles at me.

Leading up to move-in day, I prepared a list of instructions for the facility. I was terrified that an aide would tell my mom she was on mirtazapine or that a well-meaning staffer would try to get her to do karaoke. I made a list of her preferences and triggers and fears, all the while assuming no one would actually read it. I wrote it to make myself feel better. I have never been a helicopter mom to my daughter. As it turns out, I'm a helicopter mom to my mother.

I watch, astounded, during my visits. The aides have clearly read my notes.

"Your supplement," they say.

"We have good vegetarian food here. Spicy stuff, too."

"We never make anyone do activities. Some people prefer not to."

"The people here are nice," my mom says grudgingly on her third or fourth day. "Still, it will be a relief to be back home with you."

# 10

My first afternoon home after dropping my mom off, the house feels strange: bigger, more spacious. It is a new place entirely.

I don't have to listen for her shuffling footsteps or think about what I need to supply. I don't have to sprint down the stairs from my office to make lunch. I don't have to dispense her pills, plan her dinner, coax her out.

"How are you?" Noah asks cautiously. "I know it must be hard."

"Are you kidding?" I reply. "I feel great."

I always pictured the woman in the river filled with anguish. Never did I imagine that she felt free.

What does it look like when a woman chooses herself? It isn't a story that gets told often. Even my *Agi*'s original version ended abruptly. We didn't get a chance to see the outcome.

I see it then. Suddenly, I know where the story came from. My *agi* must have invented it. She told it to my mom when she took my brother to India. The story was her way of telling my mom to let go.

That was why the child in the woman's arms was a boy. *Your* agi *told me this story soon after your brother was born.* The boy in the story was him.

Birds didn't carry my brother off to safety. My grandparents did.

He didn't drown. Far from it. He grew up in India, surrounded by love. My grandparents' nickname for him was *Raja*. He was a king.

He wasn't being philosophical when he said he didn't begrudge our mom. He genuinely felt that way. So do I.

That afternoon, I clean out the guest room. I wipe down the bureau, dust the vase, pick up stray candy wrappers, remove every last item from the closet. There is no reason to clean the room that same day, except that it feels so good to do it. It is a way of reclaiming the space.

I pack two suitcases that I will bring her in a few months: sweaters, scarves. Winter clothes. I'll bring these items to her eventually, when she's ready, when, without realizing it, the place has come to feel like home.

My body relaxes in a way it hasn't in over a year. I am filled with a pleasant sense of possibility. I could go for a brisk walk with Lola. I could roast a chicken for dinner! The thought makes me laugh.

We could even go on vacation. It is nearly summer. I hadn't even realized it. It's like I'm newly sighted.

I wander outside. I stand in the backyard for a long moment. For the first time in months, I feel the sun on my face.

# 11

I t's just like with the Easter bunny, Mommy."
I've been struggling with how to explain the pretext to Zoe
so that when we visit Grandma, she'll play along with the fictitious renovation. It feels uncomfortable. I don't want to con-
done lying. Instead of glossing over my dilemma, I share it with
her. As usual, she helps me see the matter differently.

Though a fervent believer in Santa Claus and the Tooth Fairy,
Zoe has never bought into the Easter bunny.

"Like, *I* know the Easter bunny isn't real," she explains, "but I
would never say that to another kid. It wouldn't be nice. It's the
same way with Grandma. The reno . . . it's her Easter bunny."

A story can be a survival mechanism. It can also be a kindness.

# 12

*Noah and Maya are renovating their house. It will take twelve weeks. You will stay here until then.*

Over the coming weeks, the other signs from the walls of her room disappear, the ones about the location of the dining hall and the timing of meals. This one remains.

Curiously, she never asks about the work. She doesn't inquire how the fictitious renovation is coming. She supplies the details herself. "My daughter has scaffolding at her house," I overhear her tell an aide. "It is very dangerous there."

"Can you believe Maya's house had those foundation issues?" she tells my brother. "So scary! Thank God nothing happened to me!"

The story shifts depending on the day. "The Indian nursing homes in New Jersey were full." "I did several tours of facilities and liked this one the best." "I told my children it was time."

"Did you stay with anyone before moving here?" a nurse asks.

The nurse has been sent by her insurance company to assess her dementia and her need for care.

"Oh yes! I stayed at my daughter's house!"

"How long did you live with her?"

"A few days. Maybe a week."

"A week?" The nurse makes a note.

"It was nice," my mom says, looking over at me fondly. "Nice that she could help me during that time."

A week. This is what our year together boils down to in my mother's memory. She tells the nurse a story about how she decided to put her house on the market, how she found a real estate agent and sold her possessions. She says my brother moved to St. Louis. Later, I have to tell the nurse that not a word of it is true.

# 13

Certain words feel right. Others are a struggle.

*Athlete.* Whenever Lou tosses the word my way, I duck.

We form stories, tell ourselves, *I am this, not that.* The story sticks.

"It's never too late to become what you might have been." It's perhaps my favorite Lou-ism. He says it to me the day I squat three hundred and sixty-five pounds.

The number is competitive-caliber lifting. It doesn't feel real. I think of myself as introspective, a bookworm. I am Clark Kent in my mind, no matter what happens when the spandex goes on.

For a long time at the gym, I couldn't reach my goal of doing pull-ups. I was stuck at a four on the assist. I would have given up, except for a woman with dirty-blond hair. I watched in admiration as she eased herself up and down. Determined, I practiced obsessively. After weeks of effort, I finally managed to do one.

One night I hop down after doing pull-up after pull-up, just as Lou predicted. "I've always wanted to do those," says a wistful voice. I turn. It's the woman I saw before.

"But you . . . you *can* do pull-ups. I've seen you."

"Oh no." She shakes her head. "Not real ones. I use a band."

A band. I was so focused on admiring her that I never noticed the black resistance band supporting her.

"I didn't think it was possible, honestly," she says with a laugh. "Now I do. You've inspired me."

She walks away before I can tell her that she's the one who inspired *me*, that I wouldn't be doing pull-ups if it weren't for her. Maybe this is how it works. The stories that inspire us are myths. We see what we want to see.

I think back to the myth I had in my head for so long, my mom caring for a baby by herself while pursuing her career. My gullibility might not have been such a bad thing. The illusion helped me. Without it, I don't know that I could have accomplished what I did. I needed the illusion, the same way I needed to misperceive the woman at the gym.

Seeing ourselves clearly is no easy task. I struggle to call myself an athlete because it means confronting my childhood. I don't like thinking about that, the same way I don't like thinking about my mom's refusal to get on a plane for me. I want her to be the mom who did everything for her kids. That part of me, the daughter, still exists.

I once thought that there was a fundamental choice with parenthood, that you had to be completely selfless or you would be a pit of need. Now I see a middle ground.

I become myself with Zoe. I grow into better versions of myself because of her. She makes me want to do better, so I do.

The woman in the river doesn't make one choice but several. She can choose to let go of her child only to come back to her stronger. I let go of Zoe when I left the house to go to that all-night café in Seattle. I let go of her when I go to the gym. I come back to her better for having chosen myself.

I think back to what the shrink tried so hard to show me. The fight for myself was always inside, but I couldn't see it. I gave my mom the credit. I wanted so fervently to believe I had support that I built her up in my mind, telling myself she was the one pulling me through. I fashioned her into a supportive band holding my weight because I didn't want to be all alone on those bars. I had been pulling myself up on my own all along. I just hadn't wanted to see it.

The story of oneself, like strength training, requires repetition. Athletes speak of muscle memory. Changing one's movement patterns is as difficult as changing one's internal monologue. The body holds on to old versions even when the mind knows better.

It's worth noting that Louis, with his black moustache and olive complexion, bears more than a passing resemblance to my father. He's the kinder version. I sometimes think my time with him has accomplished more than therapy.

"You may not think of yourself as an athlete, but it doesn't matter." Louis smiles. "You are one."

Writer. Athlete. Mom. Some words fit right away. Others take time. What matters is that we hear the dissonance, pay attention to what makes us uncomfortable. No matter the evidence before our eyes. The story we tell ourselves always wins. That is the power of stories, but also their danger.

# 14

⚜

The answer, I think, is to make sure I don't replicate the problem.

The answer is to be honest rather than impressive, vulnerable rather than proud, real rather than mythic.

The answer is to say, "You know, it was hard, standing in that river. I didn't know how much more I could take. Luckily there was a phone. I dialed for help."

I don't want to give my daughter grand heroics she will later find daunting. If I edit my story the way my mom did, omitting here, glossing over there, my daughter will build me up in her mind as someone who didn't struggle.

"When did you know you wanted to be a writer, Mommy?" she recently asked.

"I always knew," I very nearly replied. This would have been news to my pre-med self, my management consultant self, my academic self, my nonprofit self—all the contradictory versions of me. "It took me years to figure out," I told Zoe earnestly. "Even when I kind of knew, I was scared to do it. Sometimes these things just take time."

Here is what I want my daughter to know. Here is what I want my future self to know (and by "future self," I mean the person who two hours from now will butt up against the same problems in new form).

I benefited from the support I received. I benefited from talking to the shrink. I benefited each time I asked for help.

I don't regret getting it. I regret the hard time I gave myself. I felt guilty when I could have felt free.

Myths are nice. They just aren't very useful.

# 15

"Does she recognize you?" This is the question everyone asks when they hear my mom has dementia. They picture a dotty old woman wandering the streets in a pink bathrobe, just as I once did.

My mom recognizes me, I tell them. The problem is that I don't recognize her.

I haven't thought of her as "Mom" in some time. I think of her as "Grandma" or, more simply, "her." *I have to visit her tomorrow.* I still call her "Mom" when I see her, but I do it for her sake, perhaps the way Caren once did for me. It serves as a reminder. My job is to anchor her so she does not float away. I call her "Mom" to give her a story of who she is.

By August, the last sign on her wall comes down. I don't know when she removes it. She stops asking when she will return to my house. She doesn't mention the renovation. Just like that, the pretext is gone.

By September, she is flourishing. When I visit, she's never in her room. She's out with her friends. They hang out all day, roving from breakfast to lunch to dinner. She holds court in the dining room. I leave her voicemails.

The assisted living facility is like a cruise to nowhere, forever at sea. Life is structured around meals and activities. My mom doesn't drink, but there she is at happy hour, cheering on her friends as they sing. Sometimes she gets annoyed when I visit. "I have bingo," she says.

This might be the happiest period of her life. Not only do I not recognize her; I'm pretty sure she wouldn't recognize herself. She doesn't receive bills or mail at the facility. They all come to me. She never asks about them.

What's funny about her clique is that they don't know one another's names. "My friends," she says. They flock to one another. Like children, they are delighted to share in their day. Why learn names that will only be forgotten? They remember what they need to know. "She's from Florida." "She has seven grandkids." They're off to the movies or the garden. They gossip and laugh. They are lovely to one another.

They don't object when one tells the same story a dozen times. They don't question one another's dubious claims. "I decided to sell my house after my son moved to St. Louis," my mom says. Her friends smile and nod agreeably. They tell their stories. They believe one another. What more does one need?

For so long, I feared letting go. I imagined terrible outcomes. I pictured my mom alone and afraid, unable to exist without me. I told myself there was no way an assisted living facility could be as good as the home I provided. I never imagined that it would be better.

I moved her out of my house for my sake. She benefited. She has what she didn't have with me: peers, an audience that does not correct her. I want to provide this for my mom, but I can't.

"Manish is in St. Louis now, right?" she says.

"No, Mom, he's in Connecticut."

"How is first grade going for Zoe?"

"Good. She's in third grade, though."

I know my corrections are selfish. I try to listen without objecting. I watch as she lets her fishing rod out, letting the line soar. Eventually it snags.

"Do you remember when we rented a car and drove across Europe for a month?"

"Um." I scratch my ear. "That—that didn't happen, Mom."

"Oh."

I return her to reality. It is no gift. It is a slimy fish, ugly and wriggling. She'd rather let her line fly free.

# 16

It isn't always easy seeing her. It's not just that she doesn't ask about her bills and finances. She doesn't ask about me.

"What are you writing these days?" "What did you make for dinner?" "When do you go grocery shopping?" "Do you have enough time to work when Zoe is at school?" "Do you ever miss Seattle?" "Do you like your editor?" "How are the neighbors?"

These are the questions she once would have asked, no detail too small. She would have wanted to know about every part of my life. She asked questions and I took this for granted, our easy back-and-forth, the constant availability of the magic door. Then she began repeating herself. I grew annoyed. I forgot to be grateful for her questions because I was so focused on how she forgot my answers.

Now when we talk, I am the one who listens. I try to expect nothing of her, but it is an impossible exercise. To let her talk freely would be to let her forget herself.

I miss her, but that isn't an entirely accurate statement. The truth is that I miss having someone to miss. I have difficulty remembering who she once was. Alzheimer's has robbed her memory. It's robbed mine as well.

Dementia does not yank someone away. It is a slow leech. You lose the person incrementally, subtly, so gradually that you do not register the loss at first. Sometimes I hear people in mourning talk about still being able to hear their loved one's voice. I envy those people. I envy their grief.

*Mayudi, Shanudi, Ranudi.* How long has it been since she spoke the words, the three names lining up like cherries on a slot machine? Not since Zoe was born. I won the lottery with my daughter but lost the jackpot of my mom. I lost her twice, I suppose: the actual person and the person I built in my mind. I gained new vantage points along the way.

A cheerful, merry, social woman with white hair and a plump frame: This is the woman I visit. She lights up at the sight of me. "Come, come, you must meet my friends!" she exclaims.

Often when I visit, she treats it like my first time. She attempts to give me a tour. She explains how the assisted living facility works. "People can eat whenever they want. It's not like they have set meal times," she says proudly. "And they don't force you to do activities, which is nice." She passed from freshman to tour guide in the blink of an eye.

She looks different. It's not just that she's gained weight. Her forehead is smooth, her eyes no longer fixed in a suspicious squint. Her affect, to use the medical parlance, has changed. She looks happy.

"I chose this room because it is on the ground floor," she explains. "That way I don't have to bother with the elevator."

Who is she? It is an interesting question. Occasionally I catch glimmers of her old self when I ask her about India or when relatives visit. The experiences stir her. It's like watching an old muscle get activated. *You remind me of my mom,* I want to tell her.

I miss her scowl. I miss her harsh judgments. I miss when she was arrogant, lofty, shrewd. I miss my mom.

Some of the relatives who visit are the same people she once cut out of her life, people she refused to speak to after her divorce. She doesn't remember her former grudges. I am glad for this. She sees her cousins and welcomes them, offers to give them a tour. "You must meet my friends!" she says.

Maybe there is another version of the story of the woman in the river. Maybe when she lets go, the child learns to swim. The woman does, too. Their time together in the water has made them stronger. They each paddle to shore.

I don't think I was really in adulthood until I had done this thing, sewn together past and present, reconciled the myth of my mother with the reality, held her, then let her go. I think about who she once was to me. I learn who she was to herself. I watch her recede. I find myself as she fades.

We are on separate shores now. She casts out her line and lets it fly. She is a storyteller, delighting in tales. My favorite times are when she does not know I am there. "Listen," she says, to the circle of women, the one from Florida, the one who has seven grandchildren. "Listen to what once happened to me." Their smiling faces lean forward, eager. Her line glints in the sun. The moment is perfect without me.

# Epilogue

I am sitting in the kitchen with Zoe on a winter afternoon after school. She has decided she likes tea. We sip it together, milky and sweet, while she recounts her day. She tells me about her fourth-grade math team, a funny episode from recess, the blue jays and cardinals she spotted while walking home. I listen and nod.

It has been eighteen months since my mom moved into the assisted living facility, long enough that its initial shine has passed. Her trajectory there has reminded me of my own arc in college: an initial euphoria, then the predictable sophomore slump. She is like a junior now, I suppose, neither proud nor dispirited. She has her friends. They still roam from meals to activities, but sometimes she takes a break from them to rest in her room. I might actually get her on the phone when I call her.

The facility is perched on a hill. "I can see your house from here," she says dreamily. Part of me wonders if it is wrong of me to indulge her fantasies. My acquiescence occasionally feels like defeat.

She remembers who I am, but the organizational chart has grown fuzzy. "It's too bad Ramdas died," she remarked one day. My head whipped around so fast I put a crick in my neck. What surprised me wasn't her error about my dad, who is still very much alive, but that she had spoken his name aloud. Her grasp of our relationship, once so strictly defined, has loosened. If my father does die, I wonder if I will tell her. It seems she has already mourned him.

My mom differs from other dementia patients in one key aspect: She doesn't wander. This means that she can live with the general population at the assisted living facility instead of on the locked memory floor. This also means that she is able to manipulate new staff. She convinced a doctor she didn't need Aricept. She convinced a med tech she would take her "supplement" later instead of taking it on the spot. I know because I found a stash of pills in her cabinet. "She told me she was a psychiatrist," the med tech said, sounding shaken. "She told me she wasn't like the other residents, with dementia."

Under or over? Do I err on the side of relaxing my grip or tightening my hold? It is the constant question of caregiving and parenthood. I could have my mom transferred to the locked memory floor. It would certainly make my life easier. My mom would be assigned a central caretaker who would know all her tricks. It would be a relief, but it would come with a cost. She wouldn't have her friends. More than that, she wouldn't have her independence—her story.

Perhaps the question of when and how to let go is the real lesson of the woman in the river. I think about this with respect to my mom, Zoe—even myself. When do we let go of others? Who are we when we come back to ourselves?

Only recently have I registered my own feelings regarding my mom—namely, a deep and harrowing grief. It sneaks up on me. A nurse drawing my blood during a checkup blows air on the spot after swabbing it with alcohol. I imagine my mom reprimanding her and have to blink back tears. "Are you okay?" the nurse asks, concerned.

A silly interaction with the school principal, the near accident caused by a distracted driver, the inexpensive earring I lose—these are the minutiae I once would have shared with my mom. How trivial these events, how utterly inconsequential, but in receiving them she performed a role. To listen is not inconsequential at all. Her patients knew this. So did I.

When my mom would ask, "How are you?" she meant it. I miss having someone in my life who cared about the details, who gave me the space to be an unhurried version of myself. I don't think there is a replacement for this. No one else can be a mom, provide a listening ear for every slight. It is true that I have a hard time recalling her, how she used to be, yet I feel her acutely in the space created by her absence, its particular hollow. In grieving her, I remember.

I think of her as I make my own choices as a mother. I carry on her legacy of listening when I sit down with my daughter over tea. I break from her legacy by carving out that time while Zoe is young.

Zoe opens up to me more, perhaps because she senses I am available. She asks me frank questions, which I answer as honestly as I can. I know from my mom that the hardest answers to give are the most necessary. I don't begrudge my mom for having chosen herself. I just wish that she had owned it.

What does it mean for a woman to choose herself? It means having the audacity to see her own worth. For so long, I couldn't do this. I created illusions.

I am learning to give myself credit. This, I think, was why weight lifting first called out to me. It made me claim what I had always shied away from: my strength. It is impossible to give someone else credit when shouldering several hundred pounds. And while I once would have insisted it was my sage trainer who empowered me, I now recognize that Louis didn't make me into an athlete. I already was one.

My bond with Zoe has grown. This means the world to me. Looking back, I realize that my favorite times with my mom weren't when I thought she had answers, but when we leaned on each other.

What I know now about the river is that my daughter helps me cross it. She lights the way. Because of her, I see that choosing myself helps us both. I am better for this life in my arms, more aware, more resilient. My daughter gives me life in its glorious and teeming fullness.

What I see as well is that my mom is not lost to me. She lives on in me and in Zoe. Zoe has a particular way of sitting, a position she has favored since toddlerhood. Her chin rests on one knee, her other leg folded beneath her, a pose I cannot replicate without toppling over. The only other person I have ever seen sit this way is my mother.

Zoe is her own person. She loves science, just like her grandmother, but she also loves to read, just like me. Then there are the things she loves to do that are completely her own. She will forge her own path.

We are tied up in one another, she and her grandmother and I. Like Russian dolls, we hold the others inside, the future and past bound up inextricably. I think back to those hallowed words from literature: *The past isn't even the past.* We are borne back ceaselessly. How they ring true. We move forward by going back.

And so I let go. I let go of Zoe and bring her back to me once more. I let go a little longer each time, choose myself less tentatively each time, until one fine day, we will look at each other and recognize the strong swimmers we have become. Eventually she will arrive on a separate shore. She will look back over her shoulder and see me, smaller than she remembered. I will smile and call out to her to say how proud I am.

## ABOUT THE AUTHOR

Maya Shanbhag Lang is the author of *The Sixteenth of June*. She lives in New York.